Any Questions?

Any Questions?

ISBN: Softcover 978-1-946478-40-5

Copyright © 2017 by Christopher Doyle

All rights reserved. No part of this book may be reproduced or transmitted in any form or by any means, electronic or mechanical, including photocopying, recording, or by any information storage and retrieval system, without permission in writing from the publisher.

To order additional copies of this book, contact:

Parson's Porch Books
1-423-475-7308
www.parsonsporch.com

Parson's Porch Books is an imprint of **Parson's Porch & Book Publishers** in Cleveland, Tennessee, which has double focus. We focus on the needs of creative writers who need a professional publisher to get their work to market, & we also focus on the needs of others by sharing our profits with those who struggle in poverty to meet their basic needs of food, clothing, shelter and safety.

Any Questions?

Contents

Introduction 7
Vengeful Love 13
    Ezekiel 7: 1-11; Matthew 5: 3-10

        Why does God sometimes seem forgiving and other times vengeful and angry?

Why the Bible? 21
    Job 36:16-21; Psalm 39:4-13; Lamentations 1:1-10; 1 Corinthians 13; 2 Timothy 3:15-17

        How did we get all the books of the Bible into one book?

Politics & Hypocrisy 31
    Psalm 36; Acts 21:15-25

        How can we as Christians respond to the chaos and insanity of our politics? How do we save the world from politics?

The Science of Christianity 41
    Genesis 1:1-2:4; John 20:19-29

        Why are science and religion always in competition? Why is science always trying to prove religion wrong?"

The Lord's Prayer 51
    Matthew 6: 5-13

        Why debts and debtors instead of trespass and trespassers in the Lord's Prayer?

Our Similar Problem 63
    Genesis 21: 14-18; Matthew 5: 43-48

        Can Christians find common ground with Muslims?

Such A Big Subject 71
    1 Kings 18: 1-24; Titus 3: 1-9

    The world tells us that Christianity is only one of 'many' true religions. How do we react to others that feel this way?

Little Faith 81
    Matthew 6: 19-34

    How do I get my faith back?

If Jesus Was a Jew… 91
    Genesis 29: 28-35; Ephesians 2: 1-22

    If Jesus was a Jew, why aren't we Jewish?

Idol Worship, Or? 103
    Deuteronomy 29: 15-29; 1 Corinthians 8: 1-13

    What's the big deal with the Shroud of Turin? & Why is Christ's body not on the cross in our church?

Total Depravity 113
    Genesis 6: 1-3 & 5-8; Titus 3: 3-9

    "Why do we refuse to understand Calvin's theory of Total Depravity?"

Who Is God? 125
    Psalm 9; Romans 1: 16-25

    "Who is God?"

Introduction

Like many of my fellow Generation X'ers, I was raised in the church, and then promptly left it as soon as my parents could no longer force me to take part in what I saw as a farce. In the Roman Catholic Church in which I was raised, our priest literally told me, when I asked him about dinosaurs, that they did not really exist because they were not mentioned in the Bible. At my grandparent's church, which I attended occasionally, the priest told me that my friend was going to burn in hell. I'd approached the priest to ask about homosexuality. A friend of mine had made a comment to me suggesting that they may be. And then that same priest, when the movie "The Last Temptation of Christ" came out, spent his entire homily shouting about the horrors of this film that was blasphemous to it's very core. When I asked him afterwards if he'd seen it, he told me that he didn't need to see it because he knew what it was. These and other experiences left me scratching my head. I was left perturbed as to why these men who I saw as church leaders could so readily refuse to act in a manner that I personally believed would be in the spirit and example of Christ.

In addition to the leadership of the church that often left me with more questions than answers, it was the 1980's; the decade that was more foundational for me than any other. It was then that households began to have personal computers, video games on their televisions, cable television as the standard, and church as an almost embarrassment. Who could forget the mind-blowing scandals of Jimmy and

Tammy Fae Baker, Jimmy Swaggart, Jerry Falwell and Oral Roberts. I recall the few people that I personally knew who had gotten swept-up in what the world of televangelism seemed to offer; they would actually go around asking myself and others if we were Christian. Their intonation was that being a Christian was being whatever it was that they considered themselves. They seemed to be against the very existence of various groups of people different than themselves and believed in deep lines being drawn between the sexes. And what's more, they believed that in order to be in relationship with God, that their very narrow path was the only path to follow. I personally found that pretty distasteful, as well as incorrect, and so when I would be asked if I was a Christian by them, I would answer boldly that I was not, but that I was a Catholic.

Leaving home after finishing high school, I attended an alternative undergraduate program founded by the New York and Philadelphia Yearly Meetings of Quakers. In that program, you had to travel to at least two cultures beside your own, studying your subject within those cultural and societal contexts. Mine was history and education.

Coming out of that experience, I lived in Boston for a year and then moved back to Jerusalem where I'd done two years of that undergraduate program. I lived and worked and studied, moving then to Bethlehem in 1994. Bethlehem was and has remained as a part of the area known as the West Bank. It was in the summer of 1994 when I was introduced to Hala. We were engaged a month later, married seven months after that, and then had our first child nine months later. Sixteen months after the arrival of our first, we had our second child; both of our children are now young men.

We left the Middle East in 2005, moved immediately to Iowa where I attended seminary and became ordained as a minister of the church. It had been within the previous seven years to 2005 that I began to see the church in a much different light, and also became very willing to openly refer to myself as a Christian. The Holy Land does have a tendency to do that sort of thing to people who travel there and stay for a while. That in no way means to knock or delegitimize others' short excursions to the Holy Land and how that land changes them, but for myself who had been solidly turned away from the church, ten days or two weeks would not have done it for me.

In 2011, I was called to serve a church in South New Jersey and happily went. I served there for five and a half years and was then called to a church in North New Jersey; it is in North New Jersey that I now reside with my wife and our three dogs. I tell all of this to provide reference points to what follows in the coming pages.

In the coming pages are a short collection of sermons that attempt to answer questions that were posed by my congregations. I have found that when I begin serving a new church, that to ask for questions of any type that I can then build sermons from, is helpful not only to the congregation, but helpful to me to get to know them. What they know and don't know, their perspectives on culture, politics and society, and most of all, how they theologically see the world. Without some understanding of who and what they are before arriving to them, I have come to rely on their questions to discover how I can best serve.

The sermons deal with history, theology, the Bible and the Church. They are not %100 perfect in their grammar and I know that. They are written in a script format for a couple different reasons; first for those with hearing challenges, they can have a copy of the sermon to follow along with during the regular service. I found this to be something that many really appreciated, giving them a sense that they were getting from the service more than just a fellowship/social experience. Second, if I was to simply write a strictly academic work each week, I would be putting myself and everyone else to sleep, and lastly, I try to write in a style that will allow everyone to understand; I believe in plain speaking. A couple at church one Sunday thanked me for just that. They told me that they had always walked away from church on Sunday morning feeling that they had just been spoken over, not to. The end result was that they often walked away from church feeling that they'd not gotten much of anything from the service. I've never wanted anyone's church experience to be as my church experience growing up, I feel this subject matter far too important.

My prayer is that these be helpful on some level that will promote not only understanding about some questions that so many of us find confusing, but helpful in building a healthy and productive relationship with our God.

And just one final word for instruction's sake. It is my suggestion that you first read the scripture verses that are located in the left top corner above the title of the sermon. That may seem as obvious, but the referencing gained from the Scripture is essential. The Scripture that I use is from the New Living Translation. (There are some points in which I put direct quotes from Scripture in the sermon, it's important to know from what translation.) And lastly, it will be noted that there are sermons in which I read the Scripture within the sermon or even at the end, my format is not always the same. I suggest that you look to the Scripture listed first, if there is an asterisk, know that within the sermon that Scripture should be read.

Vengeful Love
Ezekiel 7: 1-11; Matthew 5: 3-10

Why does God sometimes seem forgiving and other times vengeful and angry?

I want to first thank you all for taking my request for questions seriously, I have gotten quite a number now, although, I would always love more. And I do also want to tell you all that I really enjoy doing this 'Question Series' of lessons that we're starting today based off of your little strips of paper, and I do enjoy this for a few reasons really. The first reason is because it takes the chore of deciding what to focus on away from my hands. And I know that lots of ministers have always simply relied on the lectionary for this, thus avoiding having to choose lesson direction, but with this plan that we now have in place for a while, not only does it take some of the responsibility away from me, but with this, you all are a little forced to be more actively engaged with our service in a pretty substantial way. I just happen to think that that's pretty darn important. And then another reason why I enjoy this is that it helps me to get a glimpse at what you do and do not already have a grasp on.

When I was teaching Middle School over in the Middle East, I would get kids coming from various places and from various schools, and I could never know ahead of time just what they did and didn't already understand. I was teaching English language, and I would get kids who could hold a conversation to at least some extent, but then I'd get other kids who didn't even know their ABC's. So, like any teacher in such a situation, I would give a kind of entry test at the beginning of the year to see where they were. This whole plan of strips of paper with questions from you all really serves in the same way, and so perhaps I should ask for some forgiveness from you for treating you like my middle schoolers. And then there's one other reason why I really like starting off in this way too. And that simply is because

I find your questions to be just absolutely fascinating. Our question today that I chose to focus on is this, "Why does God sometimes seem forgiving and other times vengeful and angry?" That's a good question.

Now, I saw this question, and I knew that this was where we were going to have to start this whole thing, because this question right here really does get down into the very core issue of difference between the Old and New Testaments, and without an understanding of that difference, it's a little hard to move forward with just about anything else – especially if we're trying to understand the Bible, which I will assume is certainly a big part of us coming here.

And so, 'Why does God sometimes seem forgiving and other times vengeful and angry?' Well, if we think about God as being vengeful, where is that idea coming from? Could it be from right at the very beginning with the Book of Genesis when God got ticked off at Adam and Eve in the Garden of Eden for the eating of an apple from a certain tree? Or maybe the image comes from when God really got fed-up with humanity and decided to wipe them all out and start over again with just Noah and his family? (And I will put out here that we're simply thinking of image of God at this point, not about the legitimacy of the Adam and Eve or Noah stories.) Or maybe we can say that the vengeful image comes from the occurrence of God wiping out Sodom and Gomorrah? I'd say that that was certainly pretty vengeful. Or maybe it was from when God decided that he'd kill all of the Israelites in the desert for worshiping the golden calf, or maybe from when God wiped out whole other nations to help the people we're told he'd chosen to be his own, or perhaps it all stems from when God kicked out of the Promised Land the Israelites themselves for worshiping the pagan gods of the other people living there, letting <u>His</u> own people then be forced into some really harsh enslavement? (That right there was actually what was going on in our Old Testament lesson this morning. Ezekiel was kind of warning the people about what God was getting ready to do if they didn't shape up really fast, but then at the same time, he was actually just simply telling them that that was what was coming down the pike for them, because they had been breaking God's laws and God had had enough.)

And so, if we think about it for even just a few seconds, there really are some amazing occurrences that we learn about in the Old Testament that are attributed to God's apparent wrath, these pretty mind-blowing stories in which God seems to just be getting even with people because they were being 'imperfect', the imperfect people that God had made us all to be. And, I will add too, that it is also in the Old Testament where we hear too about how God is actually jealous and that we must fear our God or else we could receive some sort of striking punishment, and so we have to be sure to follow God's law or know that we will suffer.

But then we have the New Testament, and suddenly the image of God changes drastically. Think about that. We Christians put forth that Jesus Christ was literally God come to us in human form, and that the reason why Jesus Christ came to us was because humanity had completely loused-up their relationship with God because they'd gotten everything literally that wrong <u>in their</u> relationship with

God. Meaning, humanity had never really actually understood what God is to them, or what it is that God wants from us who are a part of his amazing creation. Ask yourself, was Jesus Christ vengeful as God was in the Old Testament, or did he speak out against such notions? Did Jesus Christ speak about love and about love being a verb, instead of just a nice sounding noun? And I know that we all know the answer to that question. When Jesus Christ was presented with a sinner, how did he react? And I think we all know the answer to that question too.

And so suddenly, our image of God changed from vengeful, angry, punishing and jealous in the Old Testament, to one which is loving, caring, warm, forgiving and reliable in the New Testament. …Now you heard me remind you all that Christ came because humanity had completely loused-up our relationship with God…and so how did that happen?

Well, the answer is actually a very long one that's going to take a lot more than the next few minutes or even today to get through, but I think it safe to say that the bottom line has mostly to do with the point that people had never had that flesh and blood perfect example to follow, that perfect example that could truly teach us what God wants us to know, before we had Christ. Christ was perfect and selfless. Christ wasn't doing what he was doing in order to gain power and prestige, he was doing what he was doing in order <u>to give</u> power and prestige, not to mention an understanding of God and an understanding that with God, fear has no place in our lives.

And that doesn't mean that the others that had come before to try and get people to know God were corrupt or backward, that wasn't the case. Of course, there had been Moses, but Moses certainly wasn't perfect, and then there had been all of the judges, but they couldn't often find the right way to get through to the people. Samuel was great, and even though he had a wonderful relationship with God, his two sons were actually pretty horrible, which kind of showed back on him in the long run. Saul, the first King, essentially lost his mind, David was really popular and loved – by God and by everyone – but if you read some of the things that he was doing, you'll quickly realize that he wasn't exactly the perfect role model either, and neither was his son King Solomon. And then after Solomon, things really just went straight down-hill from there until Christ finally arrived. People had been waiting and waiting and waiting, but they'd just never gotten there, had never gotten it. And in some ways, I guess you can't really blame the people for not understanding, everything had been turned into rules and regulations, a crime and punishment mentality prevailed in general, and don't forget that that would also have been the way the leadership of the day would have been able to keep themselves in power, as well as their people in line. So, their teachings about God had to fit in with that way of being. But then Christ came, and just turned all of that onto its ear.

He sat with people and showed them how much he loved them, there wasn't any of this 'Vengeful Love' that was kind of sort of interpreted in the Old Testament as being what God's love was really like; that stern father image. Jesus Christ came to us more as the loving, protective older brother. Although, it is true that that image of the stern father, had and has clearly prevailed with many because of our imperfect humanity that's created a very wrong picture of our God, unfortunately. Jesus Christ, God in human form, fully human and fully divine, showed tender and caring love, and in that, Jesus Christ showed the true face of God.

You know, we only read the first few verses of the Beatitudes, Jesus' famous Sermon on the Mount found in Matthew, but I think it was enough for us today. Christ's ministry was completely based on getting as many people as possible to understand the message that he was giving on that day, on that hill that overlooked the Sea of Galilee. And it was a message of love, a message that taught that God cares, and loves, and provides, and that is very different from what everyone had been believing up until that time.

And so how do we at the end of the day ask the question about that angry God image? Well, it's a difference between Old and New Testaments for sure, and a difference between an understanding of our relationship with our God through Christ, verses thinking about God and interpreting God through very imperfect purely human minds. Certainly, my hope is that we who refer to ourselves as Christians will always work and strive to understand our God, not by putting him into our man-made boxes, but by prayerfully opening ourselves up to Christ's spirit that can always lead us to a real and true vision of who and what our God can be to us. And then...of course we must act and react accordingly.

Why the Bible?

Job 36:16-21; Psalm 39:4-13; Lamentations 1:1-10; 1 Corinthians 13; 2 Timothy 3:15-17*

How did we get all the books of the Bible into one book?

I received this piece of paper right here from someone in this congregation, and this person shall remain nameless. However, I will say about this person that they are quite young, have blond hair and wear red framed eye glasses with little hearts on them. And, the question that this person, who shall remain nameless, asks goes like this, "How did we get all the books of the bible into one book?" Now, this is a most wonderful question, and one that I know everyone here has probably thought about <u>and</u> questioned about at one time or another in their lives. And I really do believe that for everyone who considers and professes to call themselves Christian, that it's really pretty essential to have this very basic information. I remember one time years ago in the Middle East, a Muslim friend of mine challenged me about my faith saying, "In Islam we have only one book – The Koran – and you Christians have all of these books and so many different versions. Just what is it that you believe?" That too was a pretty good question, and so after being taken to task about this subject I realized how important it really is for us all to grasp this point.

So anyway, I thought and considered how best to pull an explanation of all of this together in an amazingly short time frame that we have for the sermon, this subject could certainly be the topic of a complete day seminar and certainly more, but I know I don't have that kind of time, so I pulled out of a book what I thought was a pretty good and quick explanation and thought that we would start there. The book just happens to be, "The Complete Idiot's Guide to the Bible".

"Ever wonder how our Bible came to exist? Was it dropped to Earth by aliens? Was it patched together like a community cookbook? Not quite. The truth is more interesting.

Actually, the Bible is a collection of 66 books divided in two sections, the Old and the New Testaments. To write these scriptures, God chose and inspired people, gathered from all walks of life from many different eras, and employed various literary styles, such as poetry, prophecy, history, love songs, and biography.

The Old Testament, written in Hebrew and Aramaic, portrays God's dealings with His chosen people, the Jews, who were the human bloodline of Jesus. He is the grand centerpiece of the entire Bible. Over the centuries the books of the Old Testament were collected by unknown Jewish holy men and finally categorized in divisions called Law, Prophets, and Writings.

After a 400-year interval, the New Testament begins – revealing the life, death and resurrection of Jesus the Messiah (the "anointed one") and later the beginning of the first churches in Greece, Italy and Asia Minor. Much of the New Testament was originally written as letters (or epistles) to churches. These, combined with the Gospels detailing the life of Christ and Acts, a history of the church, were used to educate and encourage Christian congregations."[1]

Now that's a pretty good start, but then we get to the year 325 AD, that's 325 years after the birth of Christ, and we have lots of churches popping up all around the Mediterranean Sea and all of them are putting together their own writings that <u>they</u> refer to as the most authoritative or most truthful words written about Christ and the theology that we follow. And so then naturally arguments started between all of these communities calling themselves the church because, of course, everyone had to be right. Remember in Acts the first big argument was Who Was a Christian? The Apostles were saying that you had to be a Jew first and then <u>become</u> a Christian, while Paul was arguing that all that was necessary to be a Christian was to believe in and have faith in Jesus Christ as the Messiah. I think we all know that Paul eventually won that argument. The next big argument that came about was on whether Christ was divine or not. Meaning, was Jesus Christ actually God in human form, or was Jesus Christ human with a special relationship or mandate from God. And when I say argument, I don't just mean argument. The various groups that were calling themselves Christian were ready to fight to the death because of these issues – I'm sure that Christ was not looking down from heaven upon them very happily. So, Emperor Constantine, he was the first Roman Emperor, decided that to stop all of this arguing, all of the bishops from the various churches had to come together and finally

---

[1] James Stuart Bell Jr. and Stan Campbell *The Complete Guide To The Bible*, Penguin, New York, 1999) Introduction.

decide what it would be that we were going to put forth as our Christian beliefs. (Emperors had the power to do such things at that time.) And so, he brought all of these bishops to a little place in Turkey called Nicea. It was there that all of the bishops first really started talking to each other and openly debating with each other – in a good way – what it is that we profess as Christians. Hence, we have the Nicene Creed, pretty similar to the Apostle's Creed that the Protestant Churches tend more to use, but that's what they came up with. And then they also, by the way, started pouring through and deciding which writings, from what they had, were going to be the ones that everyone would come to and hold-up as the most holy and most complete guides to our faith. Now, the working out of the scriptures actually took about another fifty years or so to settle completely, but in the end of this process, what they came up with is what we today know as our Bible. And, I think it safe to say that they did a pretty good job. But what I'd like to really put in front of us today about the Bible is actually pretty well beyond this very basic history lesson. I've often heard of our Bible being said to be the world's first history book – that's actually not true. And I've heard it referred to as a book of folk tradition and as a book of stories and as a book telling of man's reasoning to believe in a God. Now I think we need to realize that even though it may well be all of those things, it's also so much more. I'd like us to listen to some of the verses that I've outlined here. I know that this way of doing things is a little un-Orthodox, but I do think it important to think outside the box sometimes. So please listen to the first piece that we have here which is Job 36:16-21....

I don't know how familiar folks may be here with Job, but Job is a book that we Christians have taken as our own, because it's a book that discusses human suffering – something that we all have to deal with in this creation. Job is also known as Wisdom Literature, in other words, it's really pretty deep stuff. And here in these specific lines, Job's friend is trying to tell him pretty flat out that <u>with</u> our God we have true freedom, he puts this forth to Job because he knows that when we're focused on God, we're not focused on all of the material things that we have thrown at us in this creation. Yes, <u>we were</u> having to deal with that issue even a few thousand years ago just as we are today. And a big part of that freedom that God gives us too, Job's friend explained, takes place when we're not worrying so much about our neighbors and what they're doing, but rather more about how <u>we</u> should be being led in our own existences. We can certainly care about our neighbor and we should, but it's about knowing where to draw that line and knowing that we are not judge and jury and that we are not ultimately responsible for more than ourselves and our own actions.

Psalm 39's verses are pretty deep too, Psalm's are also known as Wisdom Literature. Here these words of God…………………….. Those lines really kind of put us in our place. We so often think ourselves strong and invincible and able to climb tall mountains…. But then at some point we may just realize that our existences here aren't usually a big part of that bigger picture that we can see. How many people really have left a mark on creation, verses how many people there are? We can affect change if we strive for that, and we can certainly do it on a smaller scale, but I think it safe to say that the majority of us are living more <u>simple</u> and hopefully <u>pleasant</u> lives. I think human existence really is as frail as a breath when you get down to it, it's just kind of hard sometimes to realize it I guess. I'd like to skip over the Lamentations reading, however, I really do suggest that folks consider picking up their Bibles and reading through it later. It really is a very beautiful piece of Scripture that tells of the pillaging of Jerusalem by the Babylonians. What makes it so special is that it's written in such a way, that Jerusalem is written about as a woman who has been accosted and torn apart in the most brutal and saddening of ways. It's a historic telling, yet one written so poetically that you can literally picture the pain of it all in your mind. I'd really like us to skip over to the 1 Corinthians 13 reading. Being not just my favorite piece of Scripture in the entire Bible, these are words that are just dripping with meaning. If you close your eyes, and I do invite you to do that, and hear them very deeply, you can almost see Paul speaking these words that he prays the people of Corinth will grasp and then live. He's using the example of the churches in Macedonia and what he has seen them doing……………….. Isn't that just beautiful? I know it's probably one of the most quoted pieces of Scripture, especially on things that you can find in your Hallmark Store, but they really are worth reading through.

[**To use as a visual piece for the lesson, I piled on top of one another, many of the books from the shelves in my office, ones on theology and church history, commentaries and study guides.]

All of this today, including these books that you see up here in front of the Lord's table, are meant to carry home the message that our Bible is a very deep and very significant piece of work. I'm sure that you've heard that the Bible is the most published and printed book of all time, far exceeding anything that may come in as number two, but that's not because people for almost two thousand years have been controlled by bishops and popes and priests who have been telling them what they must believe. These words have been printed for more people than any other because of the breath that they give to a relationship that can often times be the most important relationship in your entire life. They've stood the test of time because of their wisdom speaking to any issue and any problem that a person may have or experience.

We have all of these books up here that could represent a life time of study and discovery, there's some pretty thick books up here too. But all of these are just a drop in the ocean of books that have been written about **this one** that I hold in my hands and read from every Sunday. How many books could a person spend a life time studying and still not know all of its secrets?

We know that this was the work of man. But we also know that this was most definitely the work of the Holy Spirit. Certainly, if God's Holy Spirit wasn't involved with this one, I know that we would've ended up with something far different…in fact, if the Holy Spirit wasn't intricately involved with the writing of Scripture, I think it quite, quite possible that we would not even be sitting in this place today with each other. Hear lastly Paul's words about the Scriptures as he sees them. Listen here, for the word of the Lord……….

> *You have been taught the holy Scriptures from childhood, and they have given you the wisdom to receive the salvation that comes by trusting in Christ Jesus. All Scripture is inspired by God and is useful to teach us what is wrong in our lives. It corrects us when we are wrong and teaches us to do what is right. God uses it to prepare and equip his people to do every good.*
>
> 2 Timothy 3:15-17

In the Name of the Father, the Son and the Holy Spirit. Amen.

Politics & Hypocrisy
Psalm 36; Acts 21:15-25

How can we as Christians respond to the chaos and insanity of our politics? How do we save the world from politics?

My job as pastor of this church, as I see it, is really very multi-functional. Now, I don't think that that's any new idea, and in fact I think that for most pastors it's just kind of the way it's always been. A pastor though, especially today – in today's changing church, has to be able to understand budgets, has to understand programming and development, has to be a therapist and counselor, has to be a good listener, and then, at the same time a decent speaker. We also may be called on to cook and clean, to plant flowers or mow lawns, to cut bushes or to shovel sidewalks or to paint; and then on top of all of that, the pastor of today also needs to be a pretty solid academic. The pastors of today need to be able to interpret and research and understand pretty big concepts, and then after coming to an understanding of said concepts, they have to try to come up with some viable explanations of how it is that the concepts presented can be related to the lives that we live today. That's probably the biggest difficulty in the job right there, and I say that because everyone views things differently, thinks about things based on their own personal experiences; ...in fact, I think it's pretty obvious to put out there that not one person in here is living the life of another, we're obviously all individuals. So, when it comes to looking at some concept that's found in Scripture, it becomes the job of the pastor, to try and generalize that concept to everyone's life, yet doing that without getting the concept too watered down and then lost. It's really quite a challenge, probably more of a challenge than a lot of people realize.

Now, with that said, today, we have this piece of Scripture in front of us that really kind of ticks me off, and I realize that it may not do the same for everyone. But here in front of us we have this situation in which Paul has been traveling throughout a pretty big chunk of the Mediterranean, I've included maps of Paul's journeys for people to have a kind of visual of what they were, and keep in mind that he'd been doing this all on foot, sometimes being persecuted, sometimes being worked against by others who claimed to know more, sometimes not eating and sometimes even being thrown into prison, but he's doing this anyway, and he's doing it because he believes <u>that</u> deeply and <u>that</u> faithfully in the mission that God has put in front of him. Paul is not just %100 convinced that Christ is his Lord and Savior, but he's %1000 sure, and he knows that he must let everyone else know this. And so, in response to his sense of call by God, he's founded churches in numerous cities and towns – some of them major cities, clearly making thousands upon thousands of converts, .and on top all of that, I would personally say that he's certainly the one person almost completely responsible for how the theology of our new covenant with God has taken shape and is thought about even today. I really have to say that no one is responsible for the development of the church and for the spreading of the Gospel message more than Paul, the only exception to that would-be Christ himself.

And so, Paul has clearly devoted his entire life to this mission, to his call, and he certainly sacrifices an incredible amount for the church and for this ministry, and so then in our reading he arrives back in Jerusalem after traveling now for years, all so that he can confer with the Jerusalem church leadership which is, by this time, we know headed-up by James because Peter has gone off to found the church in

Athens and Rome. The Scripture tells us that they 'cordially' welcome Paul. It's like it's kind of saying, 'Yah, they were happy to see him, I guess." He brought them money that he'd been collecting for the church, it doesn't mention it but I'm sure that they took it and said 'thanks'.

Paul gives to them a report of what it is that he's been doing and about the successes that he's had, about the Gentiles who have come to know Christ as their messiah. The elders in Jerusalem seem probably pretty impressed, they thanked and praised God for his success. And then they say, "Ahhh, listen Paul, we know that what you've been doing is good and all, but, uh, here in Jerusalem, we've been working pretty hard too, and we've converted lots of Jews to know Christ also, and you know, the people here that've converted still see how important it is to know the law of Moses. And so, our problem that we have, which is actually also now your problem too, is that there're rumors that you're going around telling all of these Gentiles that they don't need to worry about the law of Moses, that they don't need to know about all of these things that we hold so dear to us as Jews, don't forget that Christ was a Jew. And this is a problem for us because it's really making people doubt what we're trying to do. So, listen, this is what YOU'RE going to do. YOU are going to take a few of these guys who we have who want to devote their lives to Christ, and YOU are going to pay for them to get prepared for the ceremony we have to celebrate this and then YOU are going to take part in the ceremony yourself so that people will see YOU there. Maybe then people will stop giving us grief about things that they've been hearing."

Basically, what they're doing is telling Paul, that even with all of the sacrifice and that even with all of the work that he's done for this cause that they all find so worthy, that he needs to appease the forces that be – appease forces that are making problems for THEM. And the reason why they want Paul to appease these forces is because they're not sure HOW to confront these people who have little to no understanding and knowledge of what it is that Paul is doing. Instead of confronting these people, and supporting Paul's ministry, and instead of trying to educate these people as to the fact that the Holy Spirit works in multiple ways and that God is bigger than the box that they're putting Him into, they're acting fearful for what they see as their own ministries and they're really kind of using Paul as a bit of a scapegoat. And instead of acting truly in the way that Christ taught, what these people, these new Jewish converts of the apostles in Jerusalem, are doing is listening to rumors, taking them as factual and then drawing conclusions, conclusions based on false assumptions. As it turns out, Paul was never disregarding the Law of Moses, but was in fact, teaching the Law of Moses as given to us by Christ. I find this whole situation pretty sickening, and I also find this situation as pretty ANTI-Christian. All of this talk of peace and love and harmony and understanding and communication and compromise and community and family…... And here the apostles are showing Paul in this situation, that nothing has really changed, and they're showing him that they seem to now be taking the place of the Pharisees in the Temple, and they're demanding that Paul do as THEY want him to do – they don't threaten him, they kind of sort of speak to him as a co-worker, as a brother in Christ, but the meaning behind it all is actually made very clear with the consequences IF HE WERE NOT to do as they wish probably able to be pretty well assumed. I walk away from this reading feeling like I need to take a shower, it's all a little slimy, very hypocritical and very political.

You know, I think we always think that it's when we read the Old Testament, that it's there that we see the slimy actions of people toward one another, the power plays and power trips, knives going into backs, and we see people talking about their neighbors and families fighting with each other and nations splitting apart, and we say, "Thank God Jesus Christ came to show us the true way." But then we see that even in the New Testament, even after Christ was crucified on the cross and, and spat upon, that even after all of that…. that people really haven't changed all that much. That people are still ultimately the same, especially when they get into positions of power, positions in which they think they're justified in controlling other people or things.

This week's question that we're thinking about cracked me up when I got it. It was kind of written out extensively so I won't tell you the whole thing, but the jist of it was asking about what we as Christians can do to respond to the insanity that has seemed to envelop our political reality here in the United States. What cracked me up was more the extra note that was put into parenthesis, that read – "Don't preach on this – too dangerous." Okay…. I add in here that another question that came in which is really pretty similar was written like this, "How do we save the world from politics?"

You know, what I find rather disturbing, beside the state of our current politics, and don't get me wrong, I've always been pretty aghast – as far back as I can remember really, but what I find so disturbing is the idea that many have that we Christians are not supposed to be political. That we Christians are peace loving, and understanding of all people, and always outstretching our hands in brother and sisterhood, and so because of that, we can't really take political stances. And so, let me ask this. Was Jesus political? Hhmmmm….

Well, if you think that Jesus wasn't political, then you need to go back and have another look at the Gospels. Because Jesus wasn't just political, Jesus was a political radical. He insisted that the leadership be held accountable. Yes, he believed in paying taxes and doing all that's required as a citizen of whatever state you live in, remember he said give to Caesar what is Caesar's – and he meant that. He knew that if the state was not functioning in a way that was orderly and positive, that everyone would suffer; and anarchy was never seen as a positive way of life. But Jesus did believe that justice and compassion were also required to be a part of how the civil government would lead. And that if those components were absent, then it was/is the responsibility of all of us to see to it that they are a part of the policies being put into place by the civil authorities. It wasn't just the temple leadership and Pharisees that Jesus was railing against, it was the entire human system that had been corrupted by greed, greed, and more greed. If we're going to refer to ourselves as followers of Christ, then I believe that we must be political and take stances that sometimes will be counter to what the civil or church leadership are doing. Jesus never wanted us to bury our heads in the sand.

BUT, and there is a big but here. I personally have never, and will never, stand in front of you on a Sunday morning as your pastor and tell you what political stance or belief you need to have in order to call yourself Christian, that's up to the Holy Spirit. I can, and sometimes will, present you with situations in which issues of justice and mercy and grace need to be addressed. And I may even on rare occasions make it clear as to where I stand on any given issue. I believe that as your pastor, on Sunday mornings, I am more of a teacher than most anything else, and that as a teacher, which is what Jesus ultimately was, I can place before you something, but it's your decision to take it or leave it.

Outside of Sunday morning that may be a different story though, and I reiterate 'may be'. I am political, because I do believe that we have to be responsible for and to each other. I do believe that care and compassion are something that you show and act out, not just talk about. And I do believe that that is what Jesus expects of all of us.

In the Name of the Father, the Son and the Holy Spirit. Amen.

The Science of Christianity
Genesis 1:1-2:4; John 20:19-29

Why are science and religion always in competition?
Why is science always trying to prove religion wrong?"

Some years back, not long after Hala and I were married and anxiously expecting the arrival of our first child, we were told by someone that we had to get to the Church of the Nativity as soon as we could. For those of you who may not know it, the Church of the Nativity is the church in Bethlehem which was built over the manger cave where Jesus was born. It was right down the street from where we lived, so it wasn't a real big trip or anything. And the reason why we'd been told that we had to get there as soon as we could was because one of the pictures of Christ, which had been painted a long time ago onto one the tall marble columns in the church, was said to be crying. That's right, actual tears were said to be coming down from his eyes. CNN, the BBC, Euro News and all the major news stations were there, and they had these big spot lights pointed to that face of Christ. There were scientists there from literally all over the world, and I remember that once we reached that column inside the church, we went over to it, and I looked-up and I actually saw a tear come out of the corner of Christ's eye and roll down the face, it was the most amazing thing to see. The reporters standing nearby were interviewing a scientist that had been brought in from someplace in Europe I think, and they were questioning him about what was going on, asking if this could be just condensation of some sort. His reply was, "If this is condensation, why are the drops only coming from the corner of the eyes?"

This week we're focusing on such a wonderful question. And in fact, I have so much to say about this one that I really have to tell you that it's been a bit difficult for me to try and cut my sermon down so that we wouldn't be here all day, there are many, many facets to this question. The question that I received and am trying to address today is this, "Why are science and religion always in competition. Why is Science always trying to prove religion wrong?" Well, whoever wrote this question, I would like to take my hat off to you because you were well able to put down onto one small piece of paper the biggest argument that has encircled much of humanity since man first believed in any God. And I get it, how can we believe in anything that we can't touch with our own hands, and how can we believe in something that can't be logically reasoned to our own human minds? That of course is the basis for unbelief right there.

Now I started off today reading that long passage where our Scriptures begin because that is also the beginning point for so many, especially in today's world, who have such a hard time with the notion of an almighty God and Creator. And that's because many will put forth that we have got to either accept that God created the world in seven days, producing the first man and then the first woman from the man's rib, OR we have to believe in what Charles Darwin put forth to the world 158 years ago. So, do we give ourselves over to the belief of Creationism – the God in seven days theory – or do we give ourselves over to Darwinism – the theory of evolution that we humans evolved from what we know as monkeys? And it's an important question to answer I'd say, because it really can set the foundations of our faith. And I'll take it a step further, where does the church stand on this, and moreover, where does our Presbyterian Church stand on this?

About a year and a half ago, I was taking part in a forum in which this very thing was being discussed and then debated. There was a pastor there who was presenting to the group that in fact, the universe and earth are actually about 6000 years old. And he laid much of his claim on his literal reading of the Scripture story, and more specifically by tracing back the genealogies of the people who form the ancestry of Jesus Christ. He surmised, that if we use that genealogy and then also reason that God's definition of time is not our own, that the argument is quite sound and very legitimate, AND the way we should believe if we're going to claim to be people of true faith with Scripture being at the center of that belief. Now I know that most people today don't follow along with his reading of Scripture, or especially with his belief in Creationism, but nonetheless, the argument has seemed to have made many more of the questions and answers about faith in general all that more clouded and hazy. And I say that because we do tend to be a very black and white seeing type of species, I'd say for most people gray area is thought about as our area for doubt, and so this subject, I believe, is something that we really should come to some conclusions about.

Now, after this pastor's presentation, and I will tell you that this pastor and I were and have remained good friends - we've concluded that there are certain things that we just need to know we disagree about, but after he finished his presentation there was essentially no way that I was going to be able to sit still and say nothing. And that's because the Presbyterian Church, and this is so much about what I love about the Presbyterian Church, puts forth that the answer to this question we have today is not a black or white one, but rather a very solid gray one, and that gray is NOT AT ALL a color which represents doubt or a lack of clarity.

Now, I need to present two points about the Scripture first. First, that that Old Testament reading we've listened to today should not really ever be taken as scientifically literal, but rather as either allegorically, or poetically. Let me explain. If we look at those verses allegorically then what we'll be doing is essentially looking for the symbolism in those words and then seeing meanings in them that answer questions that may otherwise go left unanswered. For instance, when we think of the first man Adam, we should know that when this story was put onto parchment, that it was put down in ancient Hebrew, and that in ancient Hebrew, the name Adam, is actually pronounced Adome, and means 'man'. Likewise, Eve, which is pronounced Ehewa, is often defined as "source of life", but referred most always to mean "woman" in ancient Hebrew. And Eden, as in the garden, is pronounced Eedan, and actually means 'delight'. And so, what it is that we have in front of us is actually **a story** about how man and woman came into being in the Garden of Delights. The various elements are symbolic and not literal, and were instead created for a people who were 99.9% illiterate, yet desperately sensed a need for something that would give them a beginning point to their own story of who and what they are. And if you think about it, isn't that need such a human thing, something that we today still strive for? How many of us work on or have worked on or thought about our own family trees, or have signed up with Ancestry.com. This is a basic human need and always has been.

And then the other perspective that I wanted to put out there for you is that we can also look to these verses as poetic, as an art form, an art form that satisfies our need to know who we are and from where we come, yet an art form that's been made up of such beautiful words with such incredible imagery, that how could we not walk away after hearing those words feeling better about ourselves?

But on that evening a year and a half ago, I stood up and I just had to give the Reformed Church, or Presbyterian perspective. And it goes like this:

We put forth that when it comes to creation, that we mix our faith and science into what is referred to as 'theistic creationism'. This teaches us that God created the world, that God is the 'why' behind it all and that evolution – like explained to us by Charles Darwin – is essentially the 'how' behind God's plan. And if you think about it like this, it really does make more logical and acceptable sense. What this teaching is saying is that in God's massiveness, he puts the entire process into motion. And if this happened more than about six thousand years ago – the estimate of about how old the creation story in our Bible is, does that really change the magnificence of God? We Reformed Christians, we Presbyterians, put forth that God really is amazing, and we can't and don't doubt that, and we say that God still took his rest after he set the ball in motion, but that it might just have been a little farther back in history than the first time it was written about on parchment. And so, if this is the case, what exactly would that change? How does that idea effect our faith? I would like to put forth that I think that it actually helps my faith seem more real and legitimate.

I have the kind of mind that wants to tear things apart. Like I said to a group of us that gathered last Thursday, I believe that if you take a car engine apart and then put it back together, that you are most definitely going to understand it more. I think Scripture is the same, and I also think that what we refer to as Science, must be a part of all of that. And so, the bottom line is that we most certainly do not need to have science and religion in competition with each other.

We have men and women who are working constantly and for years to figure out cures for disease, better ways to grow crops, faster ways to travel, and more and better uses for countless things that we find in God's creation. We can't and don't deny that. And then we also have men and women who are working constantly and for years to figure out and show proof of God in our world. Do our intellects come from God, does God really take care of us, what can make our lives better with the lessons of Christ, what about his sacrifice on the cross, and His Holy Spirit that's with us always.

If I take a look at my life, and at things that have happened, things that I've experienced and have been able to learn from, well then, I can't deny that God takes care of us and provides us with everything we have – including our intellects. And I certainly have had it proven to me over and over again that Christ's lessons are by far the best ways for us to live this life. Clearly, I can't deny that Christ was crucified, that he died for me, and then back thinking about all of those things that I've experienced and have learned from; all of that makes me unable to deny that His Holy

Spirit isn't actively engaged in my life. And I will add, that I do feel pretty confident that I'm not the only one that feels essentially exactly this way.

Our church believes that we are all to work hand in hand, the scientific minded and the theologically minded, to advance our knowledge and ways of life. Hand in hand, together, it's simply up to us to see it, or to deny it if we really think we can.

In the Name of the Father, the Son & the Holy Spirit. Amen.

The Lord's Prayer
Matthew 6: 5-13

Why debts and debtors instead of trespass and trespassers in the Lord's Prayer?

What we have in front of us this morning is one of those things that effects every single one of us. Every single one of us sitting here, and every single one of us, pretty much, that lives on this planet. And the topic is not just The Lord's Prayer, as is the title of this sermon, but rather the topic is more centered on prayer itself. And the reason why it's one of those topics that effects pretty much everyone, is because prayer is something that for sure, the great, great majority of people in the world have at least some type of understanding of and perhaps even do, even if they're not claiming some regularly deep personal relationship with God. I'll explain.

From some of our earliest moments we experience in this life, we'll see people praying. We see other people doing it and we might go through the motions ourselves; the typical understanding is that it's like one of those things that's similar to riding a bike. We'll probably need some instruction to do it, and we'll probably not come away from that instruction understanding the very intricate nature of balance and motion and how the mechanics of the bicycle, as well as your body on a bicycle work, but you can nonetheless do it or at least go through adequate motions of doing it. And the almost natural understanding I think we have too, is that this learning about riding a bike, as is with prayer, is that it's just a natural part of growing into adulthood. Swimming is another one of those things. We get at least some instruction, most always in our childhoods, and then the assumption is that we'll now only get better at it, because now we have the basics down.

But if only prayer were that easy. I remember when I was young, that we saw a van pulled over on the side of the road one day, right off the highway, and outside of that van there were a handful of men all down on the ground kneeling and crouching with their foreheads actually touching the ground. I asked my grandfather, who was driving, what they were doing, "Praying", he said. And that seemed odd to me, because what I was used to seeing as praying was not Muslims on the side of the road, but rather my own action, as well as others around me, of kneeling on the padded kneelers that were attached to the bottom of each pew in the Catholic church that we attended. Another time I was at an elderly neighbor's house and their daughter and son-in-law were up from the city visiting, and the son-in-law was sitting in the grass in the front yard. Sitting there with his legs folded into each other, his hands resting, palms turned up, one on each knee. I asked his daughter who I was friends with what her father was doing and she told me that he'd recently gotten really into meditation; you have to realize that this was in the 1970's. I asked her what that was exactly, and she said to me, "He's praying". "Oh", I replied.

And then as a college student I went to the Holy Land, and I remember the first time going down to the Old City of Jerusalem and going to the Wailing Wall – that holiest of all places to Judaism, and seeing the Jews praying; rocking back and forth, rocking forward and backward. And even though I knew what they were doing, I couldn't help but to wonder why on earth they were doing what they were doing in that way. Seeing some of the men even hitting their heads into this wall that's three thousand years old, proudly bloodying their foreheads, in order to show the world just how fervent they are with their prayers.

And I can say that all of these types of experiences, and there are many more such experiences in differing places with differing peoples, had all led me to wonder just what exactly the deal with prayer could be; because most all people do it, no matter what religious tradition they may follow, or where in the world they may live. Although it does seem that the understanding of it is certainly not uniform.

Some people pray every day in an effort to be in a closer relationship with their God, and in that way their prayer is kind of like having a talk with your best friend, a kind of developing of something vital to any healthy relationship. Some people believe that prayer is actually how you live your life. I kind of like that one really. But then other people go through actual rituals and actions as their prayers, and look to their prayers as a responsibility that you take on, because if you don't do as you've been taught, well then, the consequences might not be too nice. And then there are other people who only pray to God when they find themselves in need; in need of 'something', something like a new car, or perhaps maybe in need of some sort of rescue. That type of prayer doesn't seem so fair to me though, I'd have to say. I'd have to refer to that type of prayer as a type of self-bargaining that can maybe make you feel productive in a difficult situation. There's usually always a deal of some sort being proposed, "God, if you do this for me, then I'll do something for you." Personally, I don't think we should put too much credence in that form of prayer; partly because I don't really see God as being unknowing that we rarely keep our sides of those deals we willingly make, but then partly because I just don't see God as the Great Provider in that way; providing what it is that we want when we snap our fingers or reach out to God in what can often times be a kind of superficial desperation.

And so I, like so many others, have wondered about prayer, have wondered not only as to what the effects of prayer can be, but have actually wondered just how exactly to pray, or perhaps I should say, how to pray effectively. So, I did what so many other people often times do, I found someone who I thought may have the answer I seek and I asked them. This person, an old boss of mine who I really did and do still truly see as one of the few people I've ever met that has actually lived the gospel message in some pretty spectacular fashion, did enlighten me at least a little bit. What he told me was that essentially any word that we lift-up with the intention or spirit of Christ is prayer. Ok, I guess that sort of helped, but that clearly didn't tell me how my prayer could be more or most effective. His answer was only really one part of the bigger answer I think we need when considering this. Clearly intention matters. I asked some other people too what they thought and how they approached the issue, but then one day I was reading Matthew 6, and suddenly a light bulb was turned on in my head. And I realized that the answer that I was seeking was there right in front of me, in that lesson of Christ, when someone quite brilliantly had asked him pretty much the same question that I'd been asking so many others. Clearly, I and others whom I've met, are not the first ones to wonder about this. In fact, I'll be so bold and propose that this probably is one of the oldest things that man has pondered since walking upright. So, what's the deal with prayer?

In Matthew 6, Jesus is at the Mt. of Beatitudes. It's actually not a mountain, but really just a good-sized hill on the edge of the Sea of Galilee. But anyway, he's there and there's a who bunch of people around him and he's taken the opportunity to teach this gathered group of people just what exactly it is that God wants us to understand about how it is that we should be in this life here on earth that we've been so lovingly provided with. And Jesus may have just been on a roll, but someone may have shouted out the question about prayer to him. In the Gospel according to Luke, the Lord's Prayer was Jesus' response to a question coming from one of the apostles.

But either way, in this lesson – considered one the beatitudes or ways in which to find happiness in this life – Jesus gives us the perfect form and sense of what prayer for us can be when most effective. We'll go through it:

<u>Father, may your name be kept holy/Our Father who art in heaven, hallowed be thy name</u>

In this one brief line, what Jesus is saying is that in our prayers, that we should always center our words on God so that whatever it is that we are putting before God, will show that we give praise and worship to our Creator, that our Creator is the one who does have the power to respond to our prayers.

<u>May your kingdom come soon, may your will be done on earth, as it is in heaven. / Thy kingdom come, thy will be done, on earth as it is in heaven.</u>

In this line we're expressing our hope, our hope in our faith and our hope in our relationship with God. Think about it, what could we actually hope for more than for God's kingdom to come to us. A kingdom or reality where everything is perfect, there is no cruelty or hate or self-centered greed, a place where there's only love for all that surrounds us. A kingdom where there is no fear of anything. What more could we want than perfection itself? We believe that this is God's will ultimately for us, and so it is exactly this way in heaven. Aren't glimpses and experiences of heaven on earth our hope and perhaps even what we aim for? And so, we lift-up praise of God and then express to God our hopes….

<u>Give us today the food we need. /Give us this day our daily bread.</u>

In this line, we're simply putting before God that it is to God that we rely on for whatever provision it is that we need in this life. When we use the word bread or food here we're not just speaking actual food, but about all of our needs. Bread during biblical times was always considered to be the great provision needed for life, think of manna from heaven – it was a bread like substance, but fulfilled all needs. God provides us with all of our needs.

<u>And forgive us our sins, as we forgive those who sin against us. / And forgive us our debts as we forgive our</u>

debtors/and forgive us our trespasses as we forgive those who trespass against us.

Now this line here is obviously speaking about forgiveness, that clearly God always forgives us of the sin that we commit. And so, in return for that, we should always forgive as God forgives us. Now notice this specifically says forgive. This one is a biggy for Christians because we have this tendency to think that forgiveness also means simply forgetting what someone may have done to us. I don't believe that this is what this means. We are to forgive as God forgives us, we should learn from the experience, but then we should move on and not continue with any type of animosity or ill will. If we were to simply forgive and forget, that wouldn't be as God does because we do believe in a final judgement by God. God forgives, but I'd say doesn't forget.

Also, I do need to mention, that this is where the question for today was centered. The question we had for today read, "Why debts and debtors instead of trespass and trespassers in the Lord's Prayer?" There actually is no difference at all, it's simply in how the Greek is being translated. Debt and Debtors was used in the original King James Version, but then you had the Revised Standard revised from the King James in the 1880's and those translators decided to change the wording to Trespass and Trespassers. Of course, today, there's now the movement to change that wording to Sin and Sinners. They're actually all good.

And don't let us yield to temptation, but rescue us from the evil one. / And lead us not into temptation, but deliver us from evil.

And then here in these lines, we're putting out there that yes, we need God's strength in this life that truly is so filled with the temptations that our choice of free will has brought to us. We acknowledge that those temptations are often negative, but because of who and what we are, we are in constant need of God's strength to be a part of all it is that we do and hope to achieve while here on earth in this life.

The final line that the Reformed Churches use: <u>For thine is the kingdom, and the power and the glory forever. Amen.</u>, is what we refer to as the doxology of the Lord's prayer. I grew up in the Catholic Church never saying the doxology, because those were words that would be left for the priest to say at the end, and then all gathered would state together 'Amen'. I'm sure that there's probably some rather superficial rule that's in place about it, but either way, the Reformed Churches felt it appropriate for all gathered to say that prayer doxology.

So now at the end of the day, what does this all mean? Well, I think that the Lord's Prayer certainly works as a guide for us in our daily Christian lives, and does give us a really good format in how to pray effectively.

Always make the center piece of your prayers your relationship with God so that your prayers are worship. Put in front of God what you perceive as your needs, as well as thank God for all of the blessings we have in our lives. (Something I honestly think we don't necessarily do as much as we should.) Think of those who you feel have harmed you in some way, forgive them and hold no malice toward them, don't wish them ill. And then ask for strength to deal with everything in front of you. And then simply finish it all up with a word of acknowledgment that you know that everything mentioned and more is being turned over to God to deal with. When praying in this way, I think we're pretty well covering all of our bases, but then also really being able to feel more holistically in relationship with our Creator, Our Creator who really does want to hear from us, this is how we actively engage with our God.

In the Name of the Father, the Son, and the Holy Spirit. Amen.

Our Similar Problem
Genesis 21: 14-18; Matthew 5: 43-48

Can Christians find common ground with Muslims?

When I was growing up, my sister and I, like probably most siblings, would somewhat regularly get into disagreements that could turn into scuffles. And I will tell you that she could be pretty awful, and I could get into lots of examples in which she was acting as just the most horrible sister a boy could ever have, but I'll save you from those details. I will tell you, however, that in the summer time, in order to respond to her acts of terrorism against me, that I would go outside and gingerly pick her flowers, the one that I particularly liked to bring her was golden rod. And I do admit that it was a bit of a devilish plan on my part really; you see she had horrible allergies in the spring and summer, and golden rod always seemed to bring on a fit of sneezing and sinus blockage that I knew would make her just miserable.

She would, of course, then go running to our mother crying, "Mom, look what Chris did, he got golden rod and stuck it in my face." I, in response, would declare that I did not stick the golden rod into her face. But that, would then most always be followed up to my mother with the latest example of whatever terrible thing it was that she had done to me. And so, it would go....

I was, however, I'd have to say, a generally pretty quiet kid, and as I got older that just became the reality even more. I do remember lots of kids in middle school though, that were not so quiet and who would regularly tease and abuse whoever just happened to be in their sites at any given moment. And yes, sometimes, I was that one in their sites. Some kids, like me, would generally just try to ignore the malevolence, but other kids would go to the teacher in an effort to get their abusers reprimanded for such less than admirable behavior. Sometimes the teacher would give a stern reprimand, sometimes they would actually kick the culprit out of the class, and sometimes the teacher would simply ignore the complaint. Either way, a lesson in how to treat your neighbor was not usually very forthcoming.

Then once in high school, I began in earnest learning more in depth the history of this world in which we live. Up until then there had been history lessons of course, but much of it was pretty tame stuff. Stuff like, George Washington and that crazy cherry tree and how honest Abe Lincoln never told a lie. But in high school, we started learning about things like the real horror of the Civil War and that it wasn't just a war that ended slavery, but rather that it was a tragedy in our human story that we're still feeling the resentments from today – over a hundred and fifty years later. We learned about why World War One was referred to as 'the war to end all wars'; essentially because there was such a brutality that was shown by each of the sides against each other, that conflict between nations was certainly forever changed. World War Two, of course, is an insane example of how horrible we can be to each other as well; not that Korea, Vietnam, the Civil Rights movement and countless other examples speak much better of us. If there's one thing that history can certainly teach us well, if we're open to the lesson, it's that human beings just love to create conflict and to place blame on other peoples and nations, because then we don't have to deal with the log in our own eye.

This week's question is one that a great percentage of people in our nation are constantly asking. The question is, "Can

Christians find common religious ground with Muslims?" The question does then go on to clarify itself, asking the difference between Muslims and Islamists and remarking that there does seem to be those who are more liberal verses those who are more conservative and even extremist. It's a good question and one that certainly needs to be faced and talked about; and I feel it fair to say that most of us probably don't know too much about the subject.

But, on the other hand, what I will say is that this is an area that I do like to believe myself as having some pretty good firsthand knowledge in. Having lived in the Middle East for the amount of time that I lived there, as well as my studies of Islam, does, I think, lend itself to at least some comprehension of the subject.

Now the reason why we have the Genesis reading that we have in front of us today is because it is those verses that are pointed to in Islam as foundational to their belief as to who and what they are. They believe that they are the descendants of Abraham and Hagar. Hagar is brought to the desert with her son Ishmael by Abraham at the insistence of his wife Sarah, they're then left there to fend for themselves. Death looks certain to be in their near future, but God comes and speaks to Hagar and tells her to not be afraid. That he will make her son Ishmael into a great nation, hence, we have the people who follow Islam, a theology which is clearly rooted in Judaism, as well as, influenced by Christianity. I think it important to put that out there first, we all tend to know that we're all related, but just not sure exactly how. That's the first part of the equation.

And then second, we also need to understand that Islam is not like Judaism or Christianity, in which the term for the adherents is closely following the name of the faith. Meaning, Jews follow Judaism and Christians follow Christianity. Well, in Islam, Islam is the faith, and Muslims are the followers; meaning: Muslims follow Islam. And, just like in Judaism and in Christianity (and really in every religion), there are liberal, conservative and more extremist followers.

For instance, in Judaism you have the followers of Rabbi Meir Kahane who have always believed in an extremist form of militancy when taking over lands from Palestinians. And, it should be noted, that they've never had any qualms with the idea of just killing Arabs; Muslim or Christian – that never mattered to them, or killing anyone else that disagreed with them for that matter. In the late 1980's and 90's they were really on the rise in Israel, and became such a problem that even Israel banned their existence. They are still around of course, but they're labeled internationally as a terrorist organization and have to stay pretty much underground, but they are nonetheless quite the extremists.

And of course, in Christianity we have our own brand of extremists too, probably the best known are the Ku Klux Klan, but they are by far not the only ones. I went on-line to look and see just what is out there and was actually pretty amazed by the plethora of extremist militant groups that find their foundations in our Bible. All of them preaching some particularly frightening forms of hate, as well as practicing violence, instead of following Christ's example which is what Christians are supposed to be doing.

Now, I say this all to you because the assumption within many of us here in the US when thinking about this question of Muslims and their attitudes toward countries that are not as they, is that it's often a really negative one, as if Islam and Muslims are represented unilaterally by ISIS, Hezbollah, Hamas, Islamic Jihad, Boca Horam or the Taliban, …the fact of the matter is that these groups really are just as despised, feared and seen as ungodly by the far majority of Muslims the world over, as I know most all Christians view likewise the Klan and Neo-Nazis, and countless other groups that are out there spouting hate in the name of Christ.

So, can we find common ground with our Muslim neighbors? Well of course, we are all human beings after all, and we all do have far more in common with each other than we have that's different. And difference doesn't have to be seen as a negative, difference can be seen as simply different, or perhaps even as a positive, perhaps even as something that we might be able to get together and celebrate. Imagine that? I can tell you though, that the commonalities are definitely there, it's just that we have to stop picking at the differences and then making those differences into festering wounds.

At the end of the day though, I do have to say that I see this question in front of us today as not being really about trying to find common ground with Muslims and their religion of Islam, but rather I see this question really as asking about how it is that we as Christians are to find common ground with any people we have differences with. How would Christ approach such a question? Oh, that's right, that was the focus of the New Testament reading this morning. "If you love only those who love you, what reward is there for that? Even corrupt tax collectors do that much. If you are kind only to your friends, how are you different from anyone else?"

It does seem to me that we often are acting as God's children more than we know it. When we're literally very young in years, we fight and bicker and argue over silly things that really shouldn't matter in the bigger picture of life. We most often then take that attitude and way of thinking with us into our adulthoods, but then the conflicts just get more and more destructive and harder to repair. My mother would always separate my sister and I when we got into it, and then very soon thereafter, there would be a truce and peace until the next time I felt the need to put golden rod into her face. Perhaps we should do a better job at recognizing Christ as the adult in the room whose example we really should be better at following…

In the name of the Father, the Son and the Holy Spirit! Amen.

Such A Big Subject
1 Kings 18: 1-24; Titus 3: 1-9

The world tells us that Christianity is only one of 'many' true religions. How do we react to others that feel this way?

The world tells us that Christianity is only one of "many" true religions. How do we react to others that feel this way? This is our question in front of us this morning, and I would have to say that this question represents one of the biggest 'age old' questions that has dogged people of faith since we essentially walked upright. This question is not pondering the existence of God, it's not considering the legitimacy of faith or our ability to believe in a higher power that involves itself with us in this life. But what this question is doing is presenting the conversation about what or who's god is the 'true' god of creation.

From the reading in the Old Testament today we obviously gather that this question wasn't a new one even then. We know that the Mesopotamians had had a very intricate belief system, as well as the Egyptians and then of course to the Greeks and Romans. We know that the Vikings had had a well-documented belief system also, as did most peoples. And it's kind of incredible really when you think about it, that this is something that we find in all of human history, no matter what continent or people we look to. Human beings have generally always had experience with and then cultivated relationships with what they have identified and defined as gods. So, we have the question in front of us today essentially asking, "Who is right?"

Now back in Old Testament times, we see how the Israelites were constantly dealing with this. Abraham develops a relationship with the God of Israel, in contrast to the various gods that existed then. The Israelites then go to Egypt to escape famine and clearly pick-up and meld into their own belief system elements from Egyptian theology.

The God of Israel then reclaims them with the help of Moses, but we know that they were over and over again wanting to turn back to what they knew from their time in Egypt. They eventually do get to the Promised Land, but once there, they're having this same question thrown at them there as well. We hear account after account of their run-ins with the people that followed the god Ba'al, as well as the goddess Asherah, our reading is actually just one example.

We see this morning King Ahab who had been one of several Israelite kings that had come from the faithful line of David, but Ahab, going against tradition, falls in love with Jezebel who'd been the daughter of the King of Tyre. Being from Tyre and not having been an Israelite, she naturally followed the pagan traditions of the people she came from. And love being often blind as we still say it is today, King Ahab would do anything for her, including turning away from his God, the God of Abraham. She's said to have manipulated Ahab away from his God, and away from God's prophets and priests. But as for our reading, this one is different because it presents quite a new scene.

In these verses, for the first time, we see an account in which the God of Israel is shown to be the 'real' god that has the real power, when being put up against the prophets and priests of Ba'al and Asherah, almost a thousand of them. And all of they with their two gods, against Elijah standing alone with the God of Israel, show the people the truth about the pagan gods that were being worshipped and believed in by so many. Up until this moment, we certainly see actions by the God of Israel that show his power and abilities, but those powers and abilities always seemed to be at odds and in competition with the other gods; making the God of Israel perhaps the most powerful, but not the only one which was believed to be legitimate.

As we hear from our reading, almost one thousand prophets and priests of Ba'al and Asherah cannot bring fire from the heavens to the sacrifice of the two bulls. That showed all the people that if all of these prophets and priests couldn't sway their gods to do as they requested, but Elijah could with his one god, well then obviously the God of Israel was the only true God, the only God of real substance.

And so, we have that shown and proven in those verses. But there are still far too many people after knowing that account, then and now, who have continued to be stubborn, believing that maybe, just maybe the God of Israel is not the only legitimate god. And I don't know if it was just their lack of faith, or just their stubbornness or if it was moreover a question of people just wanting to have all of their bases covered just in case. But clearly at the very least we will get from this, and from many other accounts in the Old Testament, that the people were obviously really confused about that question of who was right and what was real.

And, in stating the obvious, as I think I'm really quite good at, this is still an issue today. Not only do we have Hinduism and Buddhism, and Taoism, and Jainism and lots of other 'isms', but we have argument after argument going on about the God of Israel, still. Jews refuse to believe in Christ as the messiah, they're still waiting around, waiting for a warrior savior. And then of course there's Islam as well, and that we can't deny is also coming from the tradition of

Abraham's relationship with God. And then on top of it all, we have argument after argument within side of our own Christianity too.

When I went to college to do my undergraduate, I went to this very alternative Quaker college that had been founded by a bunch of hippy Quakers back in the 1960's. They were all very much about peace and love and understanding; they were all putting daisies in their hair. And then when I got there in 1988, my entering freshman class was only 42 students, we were a pretty intimate group, no one didn't know everyone. And in our mix there, there were two Catholics, me and one other – we both came from pretty strict traditional Roman Catholic backgrounds. There were a couple of traditional Quakers too. And then there was one student, her name was Tanya, who was from someplace in the middle of Texas, she was raised in some type of evangelical church. Well one night a bunch of us were sitting around talking and just having a good time. And then Tanya kind of almost tears-up and says, "You know, I love you all so much, but I'm really scared for you because you all aren't Christians and you're gonna all burn in hell." Well I think you can probably imagine the reaction of this group that was sitting around that for most, gave very little credence to organized religion to begin with. Most just looked at her as if she was obviously a loon – and she kind of was.

But I still remember that so well, because she was forcing the few of us who had been raised in a faith tradition to consider what she was saying a possibility because we didn't believe in the way that she did. According to her, WE were all wrong in our belief of God.

And I dare say that out of all of us here this morning, I may not be the only one to have been confronted with this notion in such a way, a notion that wasn't questioning that I shouldn't believe in God, but simply if I was believing correctly.

Now we all know that this is such a big subject and not one that can be fully answered in fifteen minutes. Probably all of us have one line of thought verses another and in some places, we'll agree and in other places we'll probably not. But, I guess the big thing that has always been in my head when thinking about this topic and really pondering on it, is that even though I know to my very core that my God is legitimate and that Jesus Christ is my Savior, I still can't really imagine having a God, and one that is said to be a loving God, that would subject part of His creation to eternal doom, while granting another part eternal bliss for having believed in his higher power in ONLY a very specific way. Some of the best people I've ever known have not been Christian, they've been Muslim and Jew and Hindu, while then at the same time, some of the most frightening people I've ever had to deal with had always fervently claimed to be Christian. And then, what about those who have never had the opportunity to be introduced to Christ? Do they just simply suffer eternal doom because of where they've been placed in this world by God? And what about the unbaptized? Is that really the key that has to be turned to get into the gates of heaven?

I will however, refer back to Paul, as I so often do. And what he said in his letter to his student Titus, I think puts it well.

> *Remind the people to be subject to rulers and authorities, to be obedient, to be ready to do whatever is good, 2 to slander no one, to be peaceable and considerate, and always to be gentle toward everyone.*
>
> *3 At one time we too were foolish, disobedient, deceived and enslaved by all kinds of passions and pleasures. We lived in malice and envy, being hated and hating one another. 4 But when the kindness and love of God our Savior appeared, 5 he saved us, not because of righteous things we had done, but because of his mercy. He saved us through the washing of rebirth and renewal by the Holy Spirit, 6 whom he poured out on us generously through Jesus Christ our Savior, 7 so that, having been justified by his grace, we might become heirs having the hope of eternal life. 8 This is a trustworthy saying. And I want you to stress these things, so that those who have trusted in God may be careful to devote themselves to doing what is good. These things are excellent and profitable for everyone.*
>
> *9 But avoid foolish controversies and genealogies and arguments and quarrels about the law, because these are unprofitable and* useless.

After hearing Paul's words, instead of worrying about such questions as we've had this morning, shouldn't we be concentrating on what we're doing right and good, instead of what others may be doing wrong? Shouldn't we be leading by example, and removing the log from our own eye before going after the splinter in others'? These are hard questions, I know, and I don't think there are any easy answers here. But I do believe that if we're sure to be faithful, that those who see us and know us, will follow, if not for the simple reason of us being a good example, then... in order to follow our way in having our spiritual hunger fed; for we're all hungry, and I suggest that we all don't let anyone ever say that we're not.

In the name of the Father, the Son and the Holy Spirit. Amen.

Little Faith
Matthew 6: 19-34

How do I get my faith back?

When I first went to seminary, there was a student there who was getting ready to graduate. He was maybe a few years older than I was, we'll call him John. And at that time, he was student pastoring at a little church not too far away from the seminary

Well, I was thinking about student pastoring myself, and so it had been suggested to me that I speak with John, and maybe visit with him, so that I could get an idea of just what it is that the job could entail. So, I spoke with him and he invited me to meet him at his church. We met there and talked for a while and then went to have lunch together in a local bar and grill. Places like that are really popular out there, you go into them and feel like you've kind of walked into an old time Wild West Saloon. More often than not there's country music playing in the background. I think we got burgers, but then in the midst of our conversation he asked me how I'd come to decide on attending seminary. What I told him was that at that point I wasn't even quite sure myself, but that somehow I had found myself there and that it did seem from inside of me that it was what I was supposed to be doing. I then asked him the same question and what he told me was a pretty powerful story.

John had been working for a major manufacturer, and he was doing really well for himself, he was a big wig salesman and flew all over the country selling their products. He told me that he was so busy that he often times couldn't make it home until the weekend and then sometimes not even then. In fact, he was so busy that his wife, who'd been his high school sweet heart, would have to meet him in-between flights at the airport some days to simply switch suit cases with him in the airport lounge. And it wasn't exactly the nicest life and he knew that, but it was his job to provide for his family and that he was doing quite well. Even though his wife was having to raise their children pretty much totally by herself. This went on for quite some time, but then after a while, as you can imagine the situation had gotten to the point in which no one in their house was happy with this arrangement at all. When he did make it home he was so exhausted that being a father to his kids or a husband to his wife was essentially the farthest thing from his mind. Sure, they had a nice house and a well-padded bank account, but there was, at the same time, just a lot missing.

One day, he's meeting his wife in the airport for one of their infamous suit case switches in-between flights, and his wife tells him that she's had enough and that she just can't live her life like this anymore, and that she wants a divorce. He tells her that they'll talk about this as soon as he gets home from that meeting that he couldn't be late for, and he takes off. Clearly, there's nothing else that he can think about on that trip while he's supposed to be the big wig salesman. He gets home and tells his bosses that he needs some time, a couple weeks, to deal with stuff going on with him. They give him the two weeks, he'd had plenty of vacation time built-up so that wasn't a problem.

He takes the time off and he and his wife are speaking about what has happened to their marriage and to their relationship pretty openly, it wasn't like they didn't like or love each other, it was just that the life that they'd come to lead was one in which loneliness, and depression from that loneliness, had <u>become</u> their way of life. His wife, who really is a lovely person, just didn't feel that she could do it anymore, it was breaking her in half. And for him, he knew that he wasn't happy too, even though he had everything a person could materially want. That kind of comfort clearly wasn't the issue though.

Well now, across the street from them lived a husband and wife, they had no kids of their own. The husband was an auto mechanic, and he did okay for himself, but he wasn't as cushioned financially as John. One day right after John took this time off, he's sitting outside his garage drinking a can of beer and thinking about his life and where it could all have started to go so wrong, and then his neighbor gets home after a hard day's work. He's dirty and covered in black oil and grease as lots of mechanics you'd expect would be, and he's clearly visibly tired. But John's kids, who'd been playing outside, see the neighbor pull in and they run across the street to see him. John's kids were all pretty young at this point; the oldest being eight or nine. The neighbor picks-up John's kids and is hugging them and they're giggling. They want to know what time they'll be leaving with him. John has no idea what's going on. The neighbor comes over to him and says hello, he'd not seen a lot of John at the house, but he invites him to go to church with them that evening.

Unbeknownst to John, his wife and daughters had been attending a local Presbyterian Church where'd they'd been invited by this neighbor quite some time before. John is pretty shocked to say the least, he and his wife both had not grown up in the church, nor had they ever had any interest in the church. He passes on the invitation, but his wife and daughters do go as they had been for some time now. The following week, the neighbor invites John to go with them all again, while his little girl is climbing on this dirty tired neighbor who his kids obviously adore.

This time John goes, and once there, he's meeting people who are coming up to him and saying hello and welcoming him in and acting just so darned happy and nice that at first it really annoyed the stink out of him. All he could wonder was, "What do these people have to be so darn happy about?" And he saw too that his wife and daughters just fit right in with it all, ...John was feeling like the ugly duckling and feeling just really out of place. He went back the following week with them all again basically because he kind of felt he should, not because he wanted to. And just like the week before, he couldn't understand what it was that all of these people seemed so happy about. And you have to realize, that at this point, John is really ripped up inside. He's questioning his very existence and purpose in life, he's watching his kids being closer to this guy from across the street who'd never bought them a thing (that was his thinking), yet they clearly loved him in ways that made him, their father, jealous. And, of course, the whole situation with his wife wasn't making his state of mind any easier. They were speaking and all, but his wife really was still thinking that divorce was their best option.

That night, he left the church ahead of his wife and kids, saying that he didn't feel real well – his stomach was all in knots. And he knew that his wife and daughters would get a ride home with the neighbors.

He got into his car, amazingly pent up inside. He's driving along down the road and all of a sudden, he just starts crying from the stress of it all, he's kind of emotionally just breaking down and feeling really raw. His whole world is just crumbling around him and he doesn't know what to do. He even has to pull over his car because he's become too upset to concentrate on driving, once he does that he just sits there for a few minutes bawling his eyes out and then, and he tells me this, he just cried out, "God if you're real, please help me. Show me what I'm supposed to do, I'll do anything, just let me know, show me something, anything if you're there, if you're real." He told me that at that very moment, he had this feeling come over him that was just calming and relaxing, like something just went right threw him and took out the bad stuff. He immediately calmed down and was able to get himself back together and to get back onto the road, he got back to his house, and he told me that within the course of that pretty short drive, that he knew what it was that he needed to do. That evening he told his wife that he was going to leave his work and find something that would let him be at home, that he loved her and that he wanted to be a husband to her and a father to their daughters. That was the first step.

He then switched jobs in the company, taking a major down grade in his salary, but he didn't care. He then became a regular church attender and became avid about studying the bible and praying for what it was that God wanted from him. And then lo and behold, a few years later, there he was entering seminary. ...And now today, he's still at that small, little country church. He's a very popular part time pastor. After he was ordained he felt called to stay there with them and they felt called to keep him. He preaches the Gospel on Sunday mornings and provides pastoral direction and care, and works with the youth, and then works part time on a dairy farm. From what I understand he's become quite the expert at milking cows, and he and his wife of just about 30 years are now very happy. And it all really started when he called out to God to make a change in his life, to give to him what it is that he needs, to give him faith if it really was something that could exist for him. John told me his story on that day and I can tell you that he teared-up on more than one occasion.

Now John had, previous to this, never been one to have faith, he had been what we would refer to as an unbeliever, someone who had never had belief to begin with. But he got it. And he may question what it is that he does and why, and perhaps even how, as we all do and should, but for John, when those doubts 'start-a-rollin' through, he just thinks back to what it is that happened to him that evening when driving down the road, and the doubts drift away, because he knows deep inside that it was clearly the Holy Spirit coming down upon him. Now I tell you this story, because the question that I wanted to address this morning that I had gotten on one of those little slips of paper is this, "How do I get my faith back?" I think the thought coming here is that maybe there's some type of recipe known that can clearly and succinctly deal with this question of faith, this question of how to regain or renew a faith once one feels that it has perhaps gotten lost. If I add two plus two, I'll get four, and then if I add in fifteen, I'll get nineteen, and then if I add in another fifty I'll get to sixty-nine and then another three, and then there I have my answer at seventy-two and now I've gotten it back. There's a little problem with that way of thought though, because the answer is actually about whether or not you're allowing the Spirit to do what it does best for us.

If you're feeling like your faith is waning, or cracked, or even lost, first decide if you really do want God to be in your life; is this something that really is important to you and why is it, if it is? Or maybe the problem is that you think it's about what God hasn't done for you as of late but should have and now because you didn't get what you thought you should, you're now questioning everything. Believe me, it happens all the time. Now where are you? Do you really want God in your life, do you really desire to feel like Christ is there walking beside you? Well then, all I can say is that you need to go to the Lord in prayer and ask Him to enter in. Cry out to God if you feel you need to, put it out there, God will respond, but you have to be truly open and willing to hear, and you might just have to be open to an answer that may just take you by surprise.

Christ says, store your treasure in heaven. What he's saying is that we need to look to heaven as the real treasure for our lives, that everything here is just temporary and superficial, and that once we realize that, that our hearts will always be filled with joy, that they'll always be filled with faith. "Your eye is your lamp that provides light to your whole body." It's about our outlook. If God is in your life, that glass is always half full to overflowing. Pray for the light! And what Christ says about serving two masters… Well what he's wanting us to realize is that if God isn't a part of or guiding what it is that we're doing, when it comes to our purpose, to our call in life, then there's something very wrong. Well then how will we ever be able to find satisfaction in what it is that we do?

And so…....

> 25 *"Therefore I tell you, do not worry about your life, what you will eat or drink; or about your body, what you will wear. Is not life more than food, and the body more than clothes? 26 Look at the birds of the air; they do not sow or reap or store away in barns, and yet your heavenly Father feeds them. Are you not much more valuable than they? 27 Can any one of you by worrying add a single hour to your life[a]?*
>
> 28 *"And why do you worry about clothes? See how the flowers of the field grow. They do not labor or spin. 29 Yet I tell you that not even Solomon in all his splendor was dressed like one of these. 30 If that is how God clothes the grass of the field, which is here today and tomorrow is thrown into the fire, will he not much more clothe you—you of little faith? 31 So do not worry, saying, 'What shall we eat?' or 'What shall we drink?' or 'What shall we wear?' 32 For the pagans run after all these things, and your heavenly Father knows that you need them. 33 But seek first his kingdom and his righteousness, and all these things will be given to you as well. Lift up your voice to God, lift up your voice in prayer!*

In the Name of the Father, the Son and the Holy Spirit. Amen.

If Jesus Was a Jew...
Genesis 29: 28-35; Ephesians 2: 1-22*

If Jesus was a Jew, why aren't we Jewish?

On this past Friday morning, I was taking Hala to her job and she asked me, while we'd been stopped to put gas in the car, if I knew what it was that I was going to be writing about for my sermon for today. I always write my sermons on Fridays, it's just the little system that I've got going for myself. And I told her that I just happened to have a question to deal with that was probably close to one of my favorites. The question was, or is, "If Jesus was a Jew, why aren't we Jewish?" Hala asked me if I knew the answer…, I told her that I did have at least an idea of where I thought the sermon was going to go. And then I asked her for her answer to the question, and she looked at me, and you have to realize that Hala is no theologian. And she said, "Well, because Christ was Christian." I kind of rolled my eyes at her, and I said, "Really Hala, Christ was following himself." "Well, I don't know.", she said and then she quickly and conveniently changed the subject.

The answer though is actually not that difficult to grasp, really. What I will tell you, in starting us off in my two-part, yes two-part answer, is that I am not Jewish – even though I clearly do refer to myself as a follower of and closely linked to someone who was Jewish, because I cannot claim to be able to trace my ancestral lineage to the land of Judah. You see, my ancestors were from Ireland and Germany, Poland and Holland…. not from Judah. Judah is the central/southern region of modern day Israel/Palestine. And I suspect, and probably pretty accurately so, that most of us here's ancestors are, like my own, from the more northern or central reaches of Europe. That may be presumptuous, but that is really just how I see the reality of us sitting here. Ancestrally, ethnically, at least most of us are not Jews.

Let me clarify this point here with the Biblical story. The story goes that Abraham – and I'm clearly going to assume that everyone knows who that is, came from the Land of Ur, that's in modern day Iraq. One day, God calls to him and tells him to go to a land that he would show him the path to. He decides to go of course, and once he gets to that place, he settles down there. That place is in what is today the environs of modern day Jerusalem. While there, he and his wife have a son and they name him Isaac, and I know that we all know that story. Isaac then had two sons of his own with his wife Rebekah; and they named those two boys Esau and Jacob, Esau was the older of the two.

And now this is where it starts to get a little confusing. Jacob decides to deceive his father Isaac who has become blind and quite frail. He goes to his father and pretends to be his older brother, and in the course of the conversation, he asks his father to give him his blessing. Translated into modern speak, Jacob is asking his father to make him the head of the family, something that he knows he really shouldn't do because that position is something that rightfully goes to his brother. Even today in the Middle East the head of the family is a really important position of influence and power. Isaac does this, thinking that he's speaking to Esau the older, and you have to understand that there really is no taking something like this back once it's been put out there. Isaac has essentially handed the proverbially very worthy family jewels over to the son that wasn't supposed to get them.

Of course, now, when Esau finds out what has happened, he naturally wants to beat the stink out of his brother. And how does Jacob the younger deal with this? He takes off and goes back to his mother and father's ancestral homeland to live with his uncle until his brother can calm down and deal with the loss. He gets to the Land of Ur, and who does he come across, but Rachel, his cousin, who he then falls madly in love with. He wants to marry her, but her father, his uncle, decides that he must marry the older sister Leah instead. There's this kind of unwritten rule that the younger daughter of the family is not allowed to marry before any older sister is married first. So how does Jacob deal with this? He marries them both! Yes, this was allowed in Judaism up until more recently.

Jacob then has children from both Leah and Rachel, as well as from their female servants; yes, that too was allowed in Judaism up until more recently. (And you thought that these kinds of stories only ever came out on Jerry Springer…) From these now four women, he has twelve sons, and for these twelve sons, God marks out twelve areas of land where they can each have their own families thrive. This was given to them when they returned to the land after being in Egypt and then escaping with Moses. There were twelve sons, on twelve differing pieces of land, …and it is those twelve sons that made up the twelve tribes of Israel, most of whom are considered 'lost' tribes of Israel.

The way that they got lost was because they had not been adhering to the law of Moses, and so God let the Assyrians come in and take them over and force them into slavery. The only two tribes that God left in-tact were Benjamin, and

JUDAH. And Benjamin was a particularly small tribe that ended-up eventually getting swallowed up by the larger tribe of Judah. And so, the people who are making up this large tribe of Judah – who are living in the environs of modern day Jerusalem, are called Jews. I'll state it once again, my ancestors are not from Judah, and so therefore they were not and I am not Jewish.

Now, I know that that seems obvious in some respects, but we have to keep in mind here that Judaism is not just a religion or theology, but also an ethnic identity, hence, the two-part answer for us today. Ethnically, I am German, and Irish, and Dutch and Polish, and apparently a little Scottish too.

BUT…. what about my theology. If people who are Jewish are those who look to the Ten Commandments and follow the Mosaic Law, which is essentially what it is that we say all Christians do, then wouldn't that make us actually be Jews, at least theologically? Just kind of not full-blooded Jews? Kind of like being maybe 'adopted' into Judaism?

Let's think about this. When I was a student my first year over in Jerusalem, I was having a conversation with this young woman who was a friend of my roommate, she was from Holland. Had been born by Christian parents, but for whatever reason had decided to convert to Judaism. Honestly, I think it was because of a guy, but don't quote me on that. And we were sitting together and having a conversation in which she was kind of interrogating me as to why and how I could consider myself Christian. Because Jesus was a Jew, and so if you're going to follow Jesus, why shouldn't you first learn to be a Jew? (She was all gung ho with what was being taught to her by a bunch of pretty rabid rabbis.) Essentially what she was doing was presenting to me the same exact argument that Paul and Peter and James were having throughout the first half of the Book of Acts. My problem, however, was that I had been raised in the Catholic Church, and so that meant that I didn't know the first thing about the bible. Catholics are great with CCD (Catholic Catechism Doctrine), but terrible when it comes to trying to understand the bible. Well the long and the short of it was that I didn't know how to respond to her, and so this whole issue became a big question in my own head. She told me things like, the only reason why the Christians had chosen to have their day of worship on Sundays, was in order to be different from the Jews who they were trying to disown. I actually called my mother and asked her about that one and she told me that the reason why we worship on Sunday instead of the biblical Sabbath is actually because Christ rose from the dead on a Sunday. My mother the CCD teacher was right, and that answer does make perfect sense too. Because God's Amazing Grace revealed itself to us on that day, that is our day of joyful celebration.

But anyway, so why shouldn't we be considered Jews then, at least kind of theologically, if we say we uphold the Mosaic law and follow the commandments? Well, it's like this, we kind of are, while at the same time, we're not.

You see, when God formed his covenant with Abraham and his ancestors, God's intention was that this people was going to become his light to our broken world. It was they that were being charged by God with the responsibility of informing the world about God and spreading his message of love and unity. Unfortunately, however, as we all know, the Israelites or Jews, decided that that was not what God actually wanted. They had decided that God really actually only wanted to be in relationship with them and that it was to them, and them alone, that this special relationship with God would exist. (Rather interestingly, that is still very much the thought process for most of Judaism to this day.)

But when Christ came to us, he taught us something very different. He taught us that no, God actually wants to be in relationship with the entirety of his creation, and that he needs the people of his covenant to take the responsibility of showing the world just what it really can be like to be in relationship with our loving creator. Jesus taught the meaning of God's law as given through Moses very differently than what the people had been teaching each other it was. For instance, they had been teaching an eye for an eye and a tooth for a tooth. Jesus pointed out to us that if that was really how we were going to be, pretty soon we'd all be blind and toothless. Jesus taught us that what God really wanted for us was that we love each other and treat each other as we ourselves want to be treated by others. And that if we actually did that, putting aside our greed and selfish nature, that life would be a much different and much more satisfying and lovely experience – instead of what it generally was and has generally remained.

What I think a lot of people decide not to realize or accept is that Jesus Christ was really something of a radical because he was a major reformer, he wanted to reform Judaism to be in line with what our God actually wanted for humanity in his creation. But people were, perhaps not so shockingly, stubborn and selfish and literalist, not to mention those who were in power positions not wanting to lose their power or what they saw as their influence over others.

And so because the temple leadership decided to be as they were, something new had to be started that would center on that new interpretation of the Mosaic Law, an interpretation of the Mosaic Law as given to us by Jesus Christ. Hence, what we refer to as the New Covenant, a new covenant created with all those who know Christ as their Lord and Savior. At first those who were following this new way of thinking and believing were called 'people of the way', not Christians. That label didn't come until Paul was in Syria and people started referring to him as a Christian because he was following 'the way' of Christ. Hence, we now are known as Christians, because that name just stuck.

And so, the real solid second part answer to our question....

> "As for you, you were dead in your transgressions and sins, 2 in which you used to live when you followed the ways of this world and of the ruler of the kingdom of the air, the spirit who is now at work in those who are disobedient. 3 All of us also lived among them at one time, gratifying the cravings of our flesh[a] and following its desires and thoughts. Like the rest, we were by nature deserving of wrath. 4 But because of his great love for us, God, who is rich in mercy, 5 made us alive with Christ even when we were dead in transgressions—it is by grace you have been saved. 6 And God raised us up with Christ and seated us with him in the heavenly realms in Christ Jesus, 7 in order that in the coming ages he might show the

incomparable riches of his grace, expressed in his kindness to us in Christ Jesus. 8 For it is by grace you have been saved, through faith—and this is not from yourselves, it is the gift of God— 9 not by works, so that no one can boast. 10 For we are God's handiwork, created in Christ Jesus to do good works, which God prepared in advance for us to do.

11 Therefore, remember that formerly you who are Gentiles by birth and called "uncircumcised" by those who call themselves "the circumcision" (which is done in the body by human hands)— 12 remember that at that time you were separate from Christ, excluded from citizenship in Israel and foreigners to the covenants of the promise, without hope and without God in the world. 13 But now in Christ Jesus you who once were far away have been brought near by the blood of Christ.

14 For he himself is our peace, who has made the two groups one and has destroyed the barrier, the dividing wall of hostility, 15 by setting aside in his flesh the law with its commands and regulations. His purpose was to create in himself one new humanity out of the two, thus making peace, 16 and in one body to reconcile both of them to God through the cross, by which he put to death their hostility. 17 He came and preached peace to you who were far away and peace to those who were near. 18 For through him we both have access to the Father by one Spirit.

19 Consequently, you are no longer foreigners and strangers, but fellow citizens with God's people and

also members of his household, 20 built on the foundation of the apostles and prophets, with Christ Jesus himself as the chief cornerstone. 21 In him the whole building is joined together and rises to become a holy temple in the Lord. 22 And in him you too are being built together to become a dwelling in which God lives by his Spirit."

In the Name of the Father, the Son and the Holy Spirit. Amen.

Idol Worship, Or?
Deuteronomy 29: 15-29; 1 Corinthians 8: 1-13

What's the big deal with the Shroud of Turin? & Why is Christ's body not on the cross in our church?

When I was growing-up Roman Catholic in Upstate New York, as I know I've told many of you before, I was a rather favored altar boy; never missed a Sunday. And there was something very real about that serving experience, very deep, and I can tell you that it was some of those very experiences that certainly cemented into place what I refer to as my faith. For instance, when I would stand next to the priest at the altar as he would consecrate the Eucharist, using those words of institution and blessing that we all know so well, there was always this just amazing sense of the Holy Spirit, this sense of awe, and it would go right through you. And I would have to say that it wasn't because I'd been conditioned to think or believe in a certain way, but rather because those experiences were of a spiritual nature, whether I wanted them to be or not. There was definitely something very real there, very Godly, and very beautiful.

If you've ever walked into a Catholic or Orthodox Church, I think you'll be able to relate to what I'm about to say, you get this kind of sense along these awe-filled lines, and it's not a feeling that you get when you walk into a Reformed Church building, as lovely as they certainly can be. But you walk into one of those churches where there's these beautiful stained-glass windows, and striking classical art interpretations of biblical scenes, places to light candles and sculpted statues of the holy family. You'll often find people kneeling in quiet, meditative prayer, and because of all of that, there really is just this sense that you get that makes you automatically whisper if you do just happen to have something to say, and it's all because there's this very real sense of the divine that you just automatically feel a deep respect for.

In that church where I grew up in Upstate New York, the view straight ahead from the altar where I'd be kind of stationed during the service, was the balcony where the organ was and from where the choir would sing; mainly just on holidays there'd be a choir. And on the wall above, behind the organ, there was this massive painting of St. Claire of Assisi, surrounded by bright, bright clouds with winged cherubim looking on, something that for sure you'd never see in a Protestant Church. But that painting, as well as all of the classical, beautiful, stained glass windows of saints, just seemed to so much more easily assist with that feeling of a divine presence. And I have to say, that as truly Presbyterian as I am, that there's still something so overwhelmingly special to me about those churches, about those spaces; they really do help most in informing their faith, helping them to realize that the relationship we can have with God is one that should overwhelm our senses.

Now this week, we return to our questions from little slips of paper, and after the intensity – so to speak – of Palm Sunday and Easter with all that they symbolize for us, I wanted to kind of lighten it up a bit. And I had two questions that rather matched what I felt I was looking for. One of the questions read, "What's the big deal with the Shroud of Turin?", a great question really. And then the other question was about the crucifix, and it read, "Why is Christ's body not on the cross in church?" That one in particular may have come from a recovering Catholic, I don't know, but once again, a very good question.

Now, I don't know how many of you may have an idea about the Shroud of Turin, it was actually mentioned in our Easter Scripture readings in the past weeks though. The women go to the tomb of Christ to anoint his dead body with oils, but when they got there, they saw that the tomb was empty, a couple angels tell them that he has risen from the grave and lives. They run back and tell the apostles who have all gathered and are still kind of freaking out from everything that's just happened, and they think that the women have kind of lost their minds. But, Peter, perhaps out of curiosity, goes to the tomb and ducks his head in and sees that yes indeed, the tomb is empty except for the linens that had been wrapped around Christ's body which were laying in a heap. Peter then walks away wondering what on earth was going on. The Shroud of Turin, are those linens that had been left in the tomb that had been wrapped around Christ's body after coming down off the cross.

The story goes that someone clearly went back and took those linens from the tomb and saved them. They were put away and most likely venerated by whoever had them. Then, when the First Crusade made its way from Europe, arriving in Jerusalem in the year 1099, the Knights Templar came across those linens and clearly decided that they would be in a far better position to take good care of these linens that had now been turned into the relic of all relics, ...only to be displaced from that lofty position by the cross of crucifixion or by the chalice that Christ would have used at the Last Supper, if we knew where those were and if they still exist. And so what is a relic? A relic is any kind of physical object that has been deemed as having been touched by the divine. This is something that could be directly significant to Christ, or to any number of saints. Oh, and some relics are believed to contain miraculous powers for healing, that's the thing that makes them particularly worthy.

The Knights Templar then take these linens very carefully back to Europe and present them to the church where they're declared real on every level, having the obvious impression on them of Christ's body, wounds from the crucifixion and all. Today, those linens reside in a cathedral in Turin, Italy, under tight security in a specialized glass case where humidity, heat and cold cannot affect them any longer. There has been a lot of controversy surrounding the shroud, whether it's real or not, but until now, the arguments and carbon dating tests have not produced a solid answer to that question. They are held-up by many, and visited by even more, being seen as something divinely inspiring, if not clearly touched by the divine himself.

Now why did we have that kind of scathing reading from Deuteronomy? Well, in those verses Moses is essentially giving quite the tongue lashing to the Israelites, demanding that they understand that God is essentially rather fed-up with how this spoiled group of children are acting and that God is giving them one last chance to be and do as he insists. Remember, he leads them out of their enslavement in Egypt, they complain that they will die of thirst because they have no water in the desert. So, God provides them with water. Next, they complain that they will starve in the desert for lack of food, and so God gives to them manna from heaven. Manna was apparently like some type of grain that would fall from the sky that would answer most all of their nutritional needs. But then they complain that they have no meat to eat, they want meat. And so then God sends flocks of quail to answer that need. Then, with their physical needs met, God calls Moses to the top of Mt. Sinai in order to give him the law that these saved people need so as to live a life close to their God. And what do they do? Moses goes to the top of the mountain and doesn't come down for a while, people start thinking that Moses must have died up there, and so they let their fear take over and.... They revert back to what they knew from Egypt, which was religion NOT of the God of Israel. They gather-up all of their gold and melt it down and make a golden calf, an Egyptian god, and they start praying to it, declaring IT to be their God. Their biggest problem, as with all of us even still today, is that they were having great difficulty believing in something that they couldn't see and touch.

And we all know what comes next, Moses comes down off the mountain to see this spectacle and essentially loses it, as does God. God wants to kill them all, wipe them out, he's just fed-up. But Moses intervenes and begs God to take him as the sacrificial lamb so as to save all of these people who he's clearly become attached to. God gives-in to his servant Moses and declares that he won't wipe them out, but... there are stipulations. First, Moses will not get to the Promised Land, he's sacrificed that. Second, the Israelites will have to wonder in the desert for forty years so that all adults and children of memorable age will die out, because they too are not being allowed into the Promised Land. And third, they will have to adhere to the law as it becomes written. And those are the reasons for Moses' stinging words. <u>For them</u>, he will not reach God's promise, and so they better not muck it up again, or else, or else they will lose what it is that God has offered to them, he will remove them from the land, and break the covenant that was made. No more idols, no more objects of worship and from now on, there is only God and the law that he gives that will bring his promise to them. No more graven images!

And so now why is it that in Reformed Churches we don't have Christ's body on the cross as in the Catholic and Orthodox churches?

Well, when the Great Reformation began, exactly 500 years ago this year, it was officially begun in 1517, there was a strict belief that the church had to get back to the original sense of what God wanted from humanity. That he wanted us to follow his law by the letter, that he insisted that there be no graven images, no idols and idol worship, that what we must only focus on was The Word of God. The first commandment, 'You shall love the Lord your God with all of your heart and mind and soul', was said by Christ to be one of the two most important commandments, well then….

So, they stripped the churches of everything that was reminiscent of those graven images, human images. And part of that was because people were praying to statues of Christ, and statues of Mary the mother of God, to relics that had been gathered over the years, relics like the Shroud of Turin, there were even pieces of wood that were put forth as relics – believed to be pieces of the original cross of Christ. People were wanting to believe in what they could see and touch, because it was easier that way. The Reformers were looking at verses, like these from Moses, and saying, "Wow, we've completely strayed from what it is that God wants of us."

And so then what did the Reformed Churches look like? Well, they were plain, no ceilings and walls painted with biblical scenes, no gold leafed columns, no statues of the saints and no images of the human Christ on a cross, and in the early churches there wouldn't even be a cross. There would be benches so that people wouldn't have to sit on cold floors, a pulpit from which the Word would be preached, and a copy of the Scriptures. Try to remember from pictures in our school books what the Puritan churches in colonial America looked like, there was no decoration and there was no real sense that that space had been truly set aside for the worship of God. No graven images, no idols and idol worship…only the Word of God.

Today, we have clearly relaxed on that a bit, we've got our crosses and some pictures, a lot of Protestant churches will have some simple stained glass, but rarely like in the Catholic or Orthodox churches. And ultimately, I have to say, that I really don't see the problem with such things in any tradition, I do believe that every tradition has something wonderful to add. And I'd have to say that I think Paul would have felt the same way.

Paul had been writing to the church in Corinth and they were questioning essentially the relevance of idols. Some people were eating the meat sacrificed to the pagan idols and others were saying that such acts were forbidden. What Paul said was, "But we know that there is only one God, the Father, who created everything, and we live for him. And there is only one Lord, Jesus Christ, through whom God made everything and through whom we have been given life." He tells the people, these idols mean nothing, they are irrelevant to our faith and relationship with our God. Eat the meat or don't eat the meat, what does it matter? As long as our focus is where it's supposed to be....

I will tell you that I do love religious art, I love the Philadelphia Museum of Art especially, they have an amazing collection there that really does inform your faith while giving a window into just how serious so many people throughout the last two thousand years have taken their relationship with their Christ. ...And so do I treasure the Catholic and Orthodox churches? Yes. But do I agree with everything they say or teach? Clearly not. That's why I'm Presbyterian, but that doesn't mean that we can't take something from all traditions to grow our relationship with God. To love our God with all of our heart, mind and soul can be expressed in various ways, just as long as it all points in the same direction.

In the Name of the Father, the Son, and the Holy Spirit. Amen.

Total Depravity
Genesis 6: 1-3 & 5-8; Titus 3: 3-9

"Why do we refuse to understand Calvin's theory of Total Depravity?"

Today's question is the type of question that headaches are made of, and I say that lovingly, I really do.

Actually, part of me has wondered if this question was posed by someone who simply wanted to collectively test us, or if this perhaps really is a deeply disturbing query for its author. The question is this; "Why do we refuse to understand Calvin's theory of Total Depravity?" I know, "What's that?" And before we really get into trying to answer this question, I will put out there that I don't know if the problem with this question of Total Depravity is one so much of an issue of understanding it, as much as it's one of being willing to accept it.

So let's dig in. In order to understand Total Depravity, we have to first realize that we're talking about being depraved, not deprived. Deprived means of course to be lacking something or going without. For instance, many children in our nation are deprived of a good education due to various reasonings, many politicians in our government are deprived of the respect they feel they deserve due to public opinion, and my wife, because of her work schedule, is deprived of an adequate number of hours to spend at Marshall's Department Store. Those are good examples that I think help us. But now depraved is different in that depraved is when someone is morally bankrupt, totally corrupted and completely unprincipled. I'll use depraved in a sentence that can help us to understand, "Many feel that a high percentage of the politicians in our government are depraved." I think that now clarifies the difference between deprived and depraved.

Now to understand Total Depravity, we have to really first understand Original Sin. Original Sin first befell humanity of course when in the Garden of Eden, Eve picked an apple from the tree of knowledge, the very tree that God said he didn't want her and Adam eating from. She took a bite of the apple and found it pretty good. She then picked another one and brought it to Adam, where he too thought that that apple was of the best he'd ever had. Of course, God then got mad at them both for doing as he'd told them not to do, and so in return, he made them subject to all of the harsh negatives that he'd originally not wanted us to have to withstand.

Things like fear, jealousy, greed, self-centeredness, malice and physical as well as emotional pain. By not listening to God, Adam and Eve, representing all of humanity, lost favor with God, and then fell out of relationship with him; that falling out of relationship with God due to their actions is what we refer to as the "Great Fall", and is why we refer to humanity as God's fallen creatures. Poor fallen man…

That is original sin. Now we can believe the biblical account of Adam and Eve as something that literally took place to understand original sin, or we can take the other well understood and accepted by the church explanation. And that is simply that as humanity developed, and moreover as our brains developed, our emotions – positive and negative – also developed. All of it the work of God, but the difference is that it took several millennia to transpire, not just a few days.

Clearly with the first explanation is where we pick up in our Old Testament reading in Genesis, and clearly those verses are taking place just after humanity has had enough time to develop after Cain murders his brother due to the feelings of jealousy he had toward him. People seem to be coming out of the woodwork at that point and there are suddenly now lots of people, and they're all sinful creatures, due to what Adam and Eve had done. And people were crazy, doing all sorts of things to each other, sometimes for pleasure and sometimes for spite. And God is watching all of this and is really just disgusted with what he's seeing, people had become really that bad, so bad in fact, that they'd become totally evil. And we all know what happens next, God then destroys all life on earth, except for Noah and his family and two of every creature, by unleashing the great flood. Life had actually gotten so low and far from God that even God found humanity hopeless.

Now from here we'll pick up the story with John Calvin. John Calvin is of course the father of our Presbyterian theology, really he's the father of Reformed Theology which is what most all of the Reformed Churches follow for the most part. But John Calvin took a look at the Scriptures and realized that humanity never really actually ever got any better from when they'd been at that low point where God decided to wipe them all out, except of course for Noah.

Noah and his family survive the flood and apparently each son goes off into a different direction to start a new race of people. But then soon thereafter, humanity is right back to their old shenanigans, but this time, God can't just wipe them out and start over again – remember he'd made the rainbow as a sign of his covenant with humanity, promising not to wipe them out again. But they're once again just horrible, and so what does God do now? Well, for a while he leaves them to themselves to kind of have a look see, to see if we'd come around on our own. Of course we don't.

So, he decided to get into contact with someone who he felt would be a godly person who he could be in relationship with – enter Abraham. God's plan is to have a people to call his own who will then do his bidding with humanity. In this, humanity will finally come around. And so he makes promises to Abraham about his descendants, promising to make them a people that will number the grains of sand on the beaches and the number of stars in the sky. BUT, as it turns out, they too are pretty horrible, they're no different than anyone else. They're greedy and conniving, selfish and self-serving, jealous and all of the things that frustrate God about this creature called 'man' that has just never been able to just get it, to just understand what it is that he, as their creator, wants from them.

God starts sending them prophets and priests who he thinks will teach them and inform them and show them the way that they should be in relationship with God. He sends them Moses, and Joshua and Elisha and Ruth and Samuel. He gives into them and allows them to have a king, because they're simply not listening to the prophets, he hopes the people will listen to a king…but they don't. So God then sends prophets on top of the kings; he sends Isaiah and Jeremiah, and Daniel and Ezekiel and a whole host of others. But the people just absolutely refuse to listen to these people that are especially connected to God; people are just that bad. In fact, the people have never gotten any better from when they'd gotten to that low point when God wiped them out with the flood.

John Calvin studies all of this history, all of this story of humanity. And you would think that if a people really believed that there is a God that looked onto us with favor and that all we had to do was to follow some laws that are especially designed for us to live a happy life, that we'd do it. But no, we crazy people refuse, because we like to put out there that we know so much better. It's like we just love to be wrong... We refuse to rise above that low point of the flood...

And so John Calvin saw this and he said to himself, "We are totally depraved. We're ridiculous, we're totally immoral creatures that seem not to be able to help ourselves, even when the perfect recipe for self-help is right there in front of us.' Total depravity is the existence that we live...according to John Calvin.

But if this is the case, then how is it that we can ever have salvation granted to us, how is it that we can ever really experience this promise that God, we say, so lovingly wants to provide us with? Well, and I know that you all know the answer to this one. The answer is Jesus Christ.

Year after year, and generation after generation, and prophet after prophet, finally God was just ready, frustrated with how corrupted and conniving humanity had become. He'd sent all of these prophets, and hardly anyone would listen to them. And so God came to us himself in the form of Jesus Christ. We say that he waited so long to come to us, so that we could really just realize how badly we need him. He came to us and he taught us what it is that our God really is expecting from us, as well as what it is that our God wants for us. And then, as a sacrificial offer of penance, as a way to present God with a sacrifice worthy enough to at least make up for some of the guilt of humanity that began with Adam and Eve in that garden, he died from his earthly life in an unusually horrific way that began with a beating that not one of us could ever fathom, and then that earthly life ended by being physically nailed to a cross. John Calvin taught that God's gift to humanity was himself, himself as Jesus Christ, the only being that could reconcile humanity to God, in part because humanity would never commit such an act of love as Jesus Christ so willingly did.

So, John Calvin's theory of total depravity: Man is totally depraved in every way, and the only way we may ever be able to experience any relationship with God is through Jesus Christ.

Now up to this point, we can all accept this pretty well I think. But where this does become a little bit more difficult, a little bit more of a head ache, is with the next step in this process. And for John Calvin, that meant his theory of election; and I'm not talking about anyone of us going out and voting on something. What an election is, is a process of selection, we all know that. Well for John Calvin, God's election is his process of deciding who it is that he will save, and it's not something that we can necessary hook into by choice, because in this theory, absolutely everything is at the sole decision of God – to save or not to save. According to

John Calvin, God has an absolute plan for each and every one of us, and in that plan we really don't have the ability to say yay or nay to it, we're either saved or not saved and it's already been decided before we're the apple in anyone's eye. In this theory, there is also no such thing as free will, if you haven't realized that. And so this is where so many theologians will differ from Calvin.

And so this is where the theory of Limited Depravity comes into play, and this is the theory that many Christian Reformed theologians, ministers and students of all ages fall in line with.

Limited Depravity teaches us that yes, we are depraved, that we are far from God and that trying to be close to God for us is a difficult effort to even attempt. We are pretty self-serving, we are stubborn, we are jealous and all of those things that we developed to be – whether from the bite of an apple or because of how God developed us. Yes, as we all know, faith is a hard thing. But where this whole theory differs, is that within this theory, THERE IS free will, and free will I don't think I really need to define for you. With the theory of limited depravity, we have the choice to follow Christ or to not follow Christ. We have the choice to be in relationship with God or not. And we have the choice to allow the Holy Spirit to work within-side of us, so as to be a part of Christ's church, and to be thrilled with how it is that we know our God blesses us, or not.

Of course, our God wants us to be in relationship with Him, our God wants us to know how we are being blessed, but as with any great relationship, it's always two sided. As my mother would always say, "It takes two to tango." Well with Limited Depravity, that's the big issue right there, it takes two willing participants; God is always willing – and we are…sometimes…. because we're depraved.

And so in answering this kind of big deep question about Calvin's theory on Total Depravity, maybe you can understand why I say that's it's not so much about refusing to understand it, but rather how willing we may or may not be in accepting it.

Calvin was brilliant in more ways than not, he was spiritual and academic and very much a political and social radical in the great tradition of Jesus Christ. BUT…Calvin was also pretty far from perfect and far from always being godly. Calvin rather openly believe that people were very much separated in the eyes of God by the race of humanity they were born into, and he also seemed to have not too much problem sentencing people to death by being burned alive at a stake.

Calvin did change the face of western theology forever five hundred years ago, but we do have to recognize that there have been many others who have come after him who we must say certainly matched his brilliance and determination. And it is to they that we must also look. To they, and to our Scriptures. The Reformed Church, we say, is always reforming, and so we look to our faith, and we look to our Scripture, and we see it differently at different times, depending on how we are allowing the Holy Spirit to work within side us.

Any Questions?

Just think about our Titus reading....

> *³ At one time we too were foolish, disobedient, deceived and enslaved by all kinds of passions and pleasures. We lived in malice and envy, being hated and hating one another. ⁴ But when the kindness and love of God our Savior appeared, ⁵ he saved us, not because of righteous things we had done, but because of his mercy. He saved us through the washing of rebirth and renewal by the Holy Spirit, ⁶ whom he poured out on us generously through Jesus Christ our Savior, ⁷ so that, having been justified by his grace, we might become heirs having the hope of eternal life. ⁸ This is a trustworthy saying. And I want you to stress these things, so that those who have trusted in God may be careful to devote themselves to doing what is good. These things are excellent and profitable for everyone. ⁹ But avoid foolish controversies and genealogies and arguments and quarrels about the law, because these are unprofitable and useless.*

Who Is God?
Psalm 9; Romans 1: 16-25

When I was young, and I mean when I was a child growing-up, I always had that typical picture in my head of who God is.

This all powerful older man, long white beard, long white hair, piercing eyes, bright shining light always behind him. And I'm sure you all know the picture I'm describing here; it's the accepted image of God. Added to that, of course, we have Jesus who is God's son; clearly a much younger person, no graying hair, olive complexion, and those eyes; those eyes that you know could always just see deep down into your very soul. And then there's Mary, also known as the Virgin or Mother of God, and then somehow as most of us often do, in some way, we picture God and Mary and then Jesus as this almost kind of nuclear family; poor Joseph always gets shuffled off to the side like somebody's uncle. But it's those three, God the father, Mary the mother and Jesus the son, who have always been to us the really important divine figures of our faith, the three that we Christians pray to. And I know that Protestants would of course never pray to Mary, however, we do nonetheless have to acknowledge that for the far majority of the world's Christians, Mary is essential to pray to because, well it is she that's known to have this just really great 'in' with God, kind of like our own mothers who are supposed to be able to go to our fathers to help us get something that we want whenever it is that we want it, same kind of thing really. And because we'll attach these very human ideas and images to our faith, we'll most often then tell ourselves that we have at least some understanding or idea of who God is. It's easy to us that way, it makes sense in our heads, we put relational images that we can relate easily to. And then in doing that, we can then feel better about what it is that we say we believe, because in most every other area of our faith, faith really doesn't always seem to make too much logical human sense. And so when I would ask as a child, "Who Is God?", I would do my best to turn who God is into that very human something that my small human mind could actually grasp.

I do have to wonder though if sometimes we don't make things out to be so much more complex than they have to be, if sometimes we don't make mountains out of mole hills when actually attempting to make answers to our questions easier. …

Well as it turns out, this morning our question is just this, "Who is God?" And I'll dare infer once again that we all here are probably pretty familiar with what our society has accepted as that standard image of God. Older man, long white hair and beard, but have you ever stopped to realize that that image isn't actually the God of Israel, our God, but rather Zeus; the Greek god that so much of Greek and Roman theology was built on? Most people who have studied theology and anthropology at any level will know that, of course, but it's really pretty interesting anyway. Zeus had been so prominent in Greek and then Roman culture as the image of the Almighty God, that that image just then grafted into our own god concept too, even though in our Old Testament, there is absolutely no description of what God might look like. Lots of descriptions of God, but none of them physical.

Think about Psalm 19 that we just heard, in those verses there really is this incredibly beautiful description of our God.

> "The heavens proclaim the glory of God. The skies display his craftsmanship. Day after day they continue to speak; night after night they make him known. They speak without a sound or word; their voice is never heard. Yet their message has gone throughout the earth, and their words to all the world."

Those are just breath-taking words when you think about them. What they're really telling us though is that if we want to know who God is, well then, all that we have to do is to look around us. To look up into the sky; maybe at a sunrise or maybe at a beautiful blue sky with just a few white puffy clouds, or maybe it's the power of a fierce dark storm, or maybe it's at night when we can just gaze up into the heavens and see more stars than we can count. In that sense, God certainly is overwhelming. Or maybe it's the landscape where we can see God too. We were driving through the Delaware Water Gap on the 4th of July on our way to our friends in Pennsylvania; and I will say that at certain points it really is just stunning.

One of my favorite things to do is out in the Mid-west, and that's to drive down a road or highway and to see these green rolling hills of corn for as far as the eye can see; and I know that that will sound weird to an East Coaster, but there really is something so heavenly about that scene.

And of course there, in that Psalm there are also words of joy, joy for what it is that we say our God does for us, and moreover, WANTS to do for us. His provision to us is certainly great. And then we put it all on the line in the verses that come next and we declare that it's to God that we ask for the ability to deal with all of the insanity of this world, all of the temptations that this world constantly puts down in front of us, temptations that so often trip us up. "Only God can give us the strength that we need", that's what's being declared right there from verse seven. In some ways, it sounds really straight forward, who and what God is to us, but then we know that we can never leave something like God straight forward.

Perhaps if we think about it though, maybe, just maybe, our God doesn't have to be as complex as we so often make him out to be; with a million rules to follow and regulations to adhere to, what God looks like and how old God is and if he really did create the world, and if my god is better than your god. I think the real question we should be asking about God is, should we ever allow such questions to really tear humanity apart as we so often do, proving that we aren't nearly as smart as we tell ourselves we are? Perhaps we just have to accept that maybe, just maybe, that God is just so far above and beyond our understanding that we have to leave it at that?

And then we come to our Romans reading, and here we have Paul answering our question, and giving us something of a tongue lashing at the same time.

According to Paul, God is right there for and with us, and he says that we can easily know who and what God is by simply waking up and being honest about ourselves and about what's right there staring at us, day in and day out. You see Paul tells us that God really isn't all that complicated, but that it really is us that has, at least in part, made God so difficult to capture in our hearts because we're always trying so hard to have God captured in our heads first. Trying to figure out who God is so that our intellectual selves will not feel insane for believing in something physically untouchable. He says that we've always been able to 'see God's invisible qualities' (I love the way that sounds.), able to see his power and divine nature. And maybe that is by looking up into the sky or down at the ground, or perhaps it's with the birth of a child or with being marveled by technology or by the feeling you get when you love.

The other part of that tongue lashing from Paul is that there's such a big part of us that doesn't really want to get to know God so much, because in that case, we think that God might kind of crimp our style, restrict us from those desires that we know are so desirous. Years ago, Paul was talking about pagan rituals that were so far away from this loving, caring, providing God that Jesus Christ was introducing us to. Paul wanted us silly humans to stop thinking only of ourselves and about immersing into what we find to be so superficially satisfying. I guess we still haven't gotten that message for the most part though.

And so who is God? What's the real answer? Well, I do think that God represents power for sure, the power of creation and of what creation contains. But then, when considering this question, I do also have to remember Jesus Christ, God come to us in human form, I think about those piercing eyes. And then on top of it all, I also think about all the people of the church who are trying their best to live as Christ taught, and I consider that God is actually living inside of them, inside of all of us really, all of us who are consciously trying to live his will while being led by the Holy Spirit….and I can't help but to know that that is God as well.

In the name of the Father, the Son and the Holy Spirit. Amen.

www.ingramcontent.com/pod-product-compliance
Lightning Source LLC
Chambersburg PA
CBHW072037110526
44592CB00012B/1450